Out-of-print $950

(Heard# 287)

61727
a/9xe

HOT IRONS

THE MACMILLAN COMPANY
NEW YORK · BOSTON · CHICAGO · DALLAS
ATLANTA · SAN FRANCISCO

MACMILLAN AND CO., Limited
LONDON · BOMBAY · CALCUTTA · MADRAS
MELBOURNE

THE MACMILLAN COMPANY
OF CANADA, Limited
TORONTO

HOT IRONS

Heraldry of the Range

By OREN ARNOLD
and JOHN P. HALE

New York
THE MACMILLAN COMPANY
1940

To

THE REVEREND A. S. HALE
who has loved the American West
and ministered to its spiritual needs
and in memoriam

to

W. D. ARNOLD
who in his saddle was a part of
western growth and grandeur

"A man who bestrides a horse must be essentially different from the man who cowers in a canoe."

—Washington Irving

PREFACE

THEY tell out West that a gentleman named Mr. Head-of-a-Cow [1] conceived the great American cattle industry when he walked through lush grasses from the Mississippi River to New Mexico. He could hardly have suspected how much fun and interest would eventually center around cattle branding, even though his descendants to this day are fire-stamping their cows with this significant sign: .

Brands developed as fast as the industry itself, became the symbols of a vast new saddled knighthood. Study of them is more fascinating than all the economics of cattledom. And more enlightening.

However, interpreters have been so busy envying the cowboy his health and freedom, and especially his good looks when silhouetted against the sunset, that heretofore they have failed to inspect him where he is sentimentally most vulnerable of all. There simply has been no adequate printed source of information on cattle brands and branding lore. Even the sanctified Research Bureau of the *Encyclopædia Britannica* could produce only a high-schoolish twenty-five hundred words on the subject when we sought its detailed report; and that Bureau's bibliography listed only seven titles, which proved to be no more than brand registries or short monographs. This is no fault of the *Britannica;* rather is it an oversight on the part of the students and authors who, while writing about the romantic cowboy generically, have simply neglected to approach him through his official coat of arms.

[1] Correct. He was Cabeza de Vaca, which translates thus.

In this volume we collaborators have therefore set a dual goal, both parts of which are admittedly high:

1. To establish a reference work, an "authority."
2. To be entertaining about it.

We contend that there is no excuse in any writing for lack of interest. Certainly in so glamorous a subject as brands and branding lore we have failed if we do not stimulate you and amuse you in some measure at least. But as to that, you are the jury.

As to our first goal, we shall be more contentious. Doubtless errors will be noted although we have labored to make this an accurate book and a reasonably comprehensive one. Friendly advisers first thought we should make it exhaustive, but when they discovered that Colorado alone had *twelve thousand* cattle brands registered as early as 1885—each with a story behind it—they admitted the hopelessness of our trying to set down everything. Therefore if some exciting chapter of brand history is condensed, some important personality barely named, or some significant brand not even mentioned, remember that the subject is as big as the whole western concept of life, and that we have here tightened the information down to what we feel is a usable, assimilable form.

Finally, it delights us immensely to produce the work at this particular time, in the Southwest's cuarto-centennial celebration—it is just four centuries since the *first* cattlemen came into what is now the United States of America, setting precedents in sentiment and self-reliance that are still being followed.

OREN ARNOLD
JOHN P. HALE

Phoenix, Arizona
1940

CONTENTS

HOT IRONS

CHAPTER I

HOME ON *YOUR* RANGE

Let us assume that you have a cow.

It is then fair to expect that your neighbor on the west has a cow too, and your neighbor on the north and south and east, and your neighbor who lives over the hill.

Moreover, the cows all look remarkably alike. Each has two horns, a hairy coat, four hoofs, a tail with cockleburs in it, and a voice that goes "Oom-BAW-W-W-W!" But even so, you feel that your cow is better than any of the others, and you very much want to know yours when you see it, or when you decide to sell it. What are you going to do about that?

You could, to be sure, tie a pink ribbon around yours. But you will realize that this is a hypothetical cow, which in reality is not one, but is one hundred or one thousand or one hundred thousand individuals. So the ribbon is out. Anyhow ribbons wouldn't seem ethical, or appropriate.

You might consider building a strong fence. For literally one cow, or even for a few dozen, you could build a fence around a big enough pasture. Some people even build fences around very large herds. But—fences are costly, and cows often break out anyway. Suppose your cow and the neighbors' cows broke out and—being gregarious—huddled together somewhere. No, fencing isn't enough.

So, what *can* you do?

Well, you can brand. With a red-hot iron.

If your name were Ed Doe or Sue Roe you could reasonably burn the whole name on the side of your cow, just as you sign the whole thing on your letters. Unfortunately, however, most of us are named Aloysius P. McGillicuddy or Cleopatra Abrahamson, or words to that effect, and the inconvenience of it is obvious. From this fundamental fact has sprung the custom of branding with variable monograms.

You therefore design an exclusive figure of perhaps one or two or three initials or characters, so arranged that it can be burned on quickly and recognized instantly. You make it into an iron, heat it and slap it on. Then you just stay home and play your guitar, or something, and wait until the bad weather clears up before you repair your broken fence. For even if 'your cow does go now to join the neighbors' cows, you can identify yours any time you want to.

Identification, however, is not your only major problem as a cow owner. It is just one of two. In the course of bovine events some cows necessarily are of masculine gender, and as such are endowed with sundry traits of character traceable to glands. In short, your gentleman cow [1] will inevitably develop ideas; he will reach that stage when he tears through fences to visit the lady cows. Your neighbors will resent this (even if the lady cows do not) because like as not your neighbors do not want your particular bull to father their cows' calves. You could of course build a very strong fence and keep one bull at home, but he will paw dirt and snort and romp around so that his muscles become tough and he will not be very good meat

---

[1] This will at first confuse the stranger and offend the purist, but in many instances we shall deliberately stick to the vernacular of the range. Out West, *cows* means *cattle*, referring to both male and female. If we chose to be finicky about it, *cowboy* itself would have to become *cattleboy!*

when you sell him, and so will not bring a good price. The solution for all this is to make your bull a eunuch in the first place. A bovine eunuch, in the nomenclature of the range, is a *steer*. A steer is fat and lazy, and tender; the more fat steers you have, the more money you will have in the bank for Christmas.

Castrating, therefore, is the other major problem in dealing with your cow. It is closely associated with branding and so will be taken up elsewhere in this book, but because it is the less lovely of the two processes we will hide it in a middle chapter and get along now with our main romantic theme.

If you have never lived on the rangeland you can have only a vague idea of the process of branding. We mentioned above that, if you have a cow, you can brand—saying it rather casually. This was misleading. Branding is not a simple task to be delegated to the children. Branding is not taught adequately in any school, except that of experience. Branding is not demonstrated in the Madison Square Garden Rodeo, where most spectators think they can learn all about cows and cowboys. Branding is not learned by wealthy city dudes who hang on the corral fence and watch real cow-folk at work.

There are two main circumstances under which cattle acquire their indelible monograms, and this discussion will seem vague or even silly unless you thoroughly envision the setting for each of them. In our hypothesis we must not only assume that you have a cow; we must also transplant you to a beautiful if vast and strange arena, where you, a city resident, will be temporarily as bewildered as your cow would be if suddenly turned loose in Times Square.

.   .   .   .

Around Los Angeles, Californians call an acre with a few chickens and vegetables a "ranch." Texas and Arizona wouldn't consider an acre room enough even for a hitching post.

The typical western ranch is so big that you can get lost on it if you are a tenderfoot, and sometimes even its owner gets lost. A Westchester golf course would be all right for one corner—over there where they nurse the baby colts, or perhaps where they isolate a stallion with distemper—but a real western ranch may include ten miles of flat land, a river, several creeks, and a half of a mountain range. Sometimes it is bigger than a big county. The very biggest of all (King Ranch, in Texas) is so large that between its north and south boundaries there is a month's difference in climate.

If you read this ensconced in pillows and Persian rugs in a Manhattan apartment building, you will feel sure that we are exaggerating. For bulk your criterion is Rockefeller Center; for height, the Empire State Building; for space, Central Park. It is hard to make you envision Superstition Mountain in Arizona, Pike's Peak in Colorado, or the Cross S cattle range. If you yelled "Yippeee-e-e-e!" out your window now, thousands of people—including a policeman, surely!—would hear you; but sometimes a cowboy yells yippeee-e-e-e-e just from sheer loneliness, just to hear any human voice, knowing that his is the only one in two or three days of riding distance. Wildcats, deer, antelope, cougars, bears, turkeys and such denizens still roam many parts of the West as undisturbed as they were in Buffalo Bill's day, or indeed when Columbus sailed.

With that in mind, let us now assume (again!) that you can ride a horse.

We do not mean ride the Park Trails. We are not referring now to "equitation" and "posting" and such poppycock. We mean, dammit, *riding*—the cowboy kind, whereby you can sit comfortably in a rocking saddle all day long without ever having had a riding master coach you at $5 an hour.

Imagine that you are setting out this morning—it'll be at 4 or 5 A.M., too, not 10 or 11—to inspect the ranch you have just purchased. Imagine it is in Arizona, the state that is fifth in size and about forty-fifth in population, and that, thanks to such romanticists as Zane Grey and Harold Bell Wright, is universally regarded as the wildest cowboy state. It is February, and the ranch cook, who has an alarm clock, has aroused you along with all the hands.

Your ranch house, of highly picturesque adobe mud bricks and *vigas* and rocks and all the architectural trimmings inherited from the Indians and pioneer Spaniards, backs up into a rock canyon that faces south. You come outside marveling at how warm the air is, for a February night. Oh, it is chilly, all right, maybe a degree or two below freezing, but there is none of that biting, killing sub-zero business you have been experiencing in the northern city. You take a deep breath and say, Isn't life wonderful? Glancing up, you note that the stars are almost intrusive with their brilliance, and you feel as if you could stroke the blue-black velvet of the sky. The great hulk to the east suddenly frightens you. Goodness, you had almost forgotten that cliff! Eleven hundred feet of red rock, touched here and there with green mesquite and cacti, so straight up that it seems by day to overhang, and by night to hover protectively over the ranch house, dwarfing it to doll-like proportions. That cliff is the nearest thing to a skyscraper you will ever see in your new homeland.

Your moment of reverie is interrupted then by a noise to which you are not accustomed.

"Ne-e-e-e-e-a-a-a!" it comes in a friendly whinny, and you realize it is your horse. You go down to the corral, and even in the darkness you see the scar on his rump. ♡♡ That's right, you now own the Two Hearts range. Two hearts, interlocked. Sentiment? Surely. Old John Tormey waggoned west when he was young, brought his bride on their honeymoon, homesteaded this very spot and used this very ranch house as a fortress against Apache Indians. Once the bride shot the redskin who was about to scalp her young husband. John loved her tenderly, passionately, devotedly; later registered his love on the books of Arizona Territory as the Two Hearts Brand, and for four decades burned it on his cows, horses, saddles, harness, wagons, and reputation. You have bought the Two Hearts ranch from old John's modern grandson, who foolishly wanted to move back East. You pat your horse's shoulder and put a saddle on him.

"Come an' git it, er I'll throw it to th' dogs!"

You hear this amazing statement shouted now from the shack where your cowboys dwell. Curious, you join the eight or ten other men who also have been up and stirring, hasten over and discover that the call means simply that breakfast is served. Your grizzled old ranch cook, an ex-cowboy too old for riding, has produced long slices of thick fried bacon, a pitcher of thick syrup, a platter rounded with thick hot biscuits, a two-gallon pot of black coffee and some tins of condensed milk. You sit before this, at a plain plank table.

"You takin' yore ride this mawnin', boss?" your foreman asks sociably, while eating.

You nod. Your own mouth is full, and you have latent scruples about speaking with food in your mouth.

"I'll just ride with you, I guess. Been aimin' to look at that upper eight hundred anyhow."

You don't understand him. Eight hundred what? But you don't say anything except to express pleasure at his coming. In truth, you really are glad, for you have sensed that you might need a guide and an informant while inspecting your property. But your astute foreman was two jumps ahead of you. *He* knew doggone well you would need a guide and an informant, and a protector as well, and he didn't trust any of his hands to fill that position for the new boss.

The two of you ride then for more than three hours on the almost level desert part of your ranch. It is called a desert even in the geographies and on the maps, for your ranch borders on that vast arid southern half of Arizona. However, you wonder why it is called desert. At times you can hardly ride for the tangle of mesquite and ironwood, palo verde and saguaro and cholla and prickly pear. You note—at your foreman's tactful direction—that much grass is to be seen, some of it green here even in February. The cattle you come across look well fed. Up one long and rather deep arroyo, with running water in it, you find a herd of more than a hundred cows and calves. You notice that a great many of them bear no brand or other mark. The calves, though, are sucking Two Hearts cows.

You circle around a mountain, the horses going at a steady walk, and note several water courses or canyons leading to higher ground. You take one of these, and get into rougher going. When you have climbed for a long while your horse shows signs of exhaustion. So do you, for that matter. Moreover, thirst has claimed your attention. And—it must be getting near noon!

When you have circled for a half hour longer, still climbing, the air is much colder, the hunger is growing, the thirst is painful. Then the foreman speaks.

"Spring water right under the hump yonder," says he. "I could use some of it."

So could you! Never before has water tasted so delicious, although it is your first experience at drinking from a cupped hat brim. You men and the horses are all revived. The horses start cropping grass.

"I stuck in a little grub," the foreman says then.

My Lord, you groan inwardly, the thought never occurred to me!

No. You had been going for a canter in the Park, or something like that. But your wise foreman has anticipated you again. He produces some of the heavy biscuits you saw at breakfast. They have been opened and sopped in the syrup. They are congealed, rather packy and cold now, but no harder nor colder than the flour-fried beefsteak which was left over from supper the night before, and which has been brought along also. The food has all been wrapped in a big rag and has ridden all morning in a saddle sling. It is mashed, but identifiable.

You, who have paid as high as ten dollars for a meal at the Waldorf, and eaten the choicest daintiest viands of Europe, sit down cross-legged on mother earth and pitch in. Willingly, enthusiastically. Nor can you now conceive of any other food anywhere tasting half as good as this.

A few bits and scraps are left, and these are carefully stored back in the saddle sling. You roll a cigarette from your foreman's sack—your first effort at rolling, which he diplomatically ignores; then you ride on. The talk has shifted to a serious study of soil conditions, probable grass growth, underbrush which can furnish some stock browse in emergency, waterholes, roundup requirements, and a hundred such things. Mostly you do the listening, probing with a few questions.

This keeps up as you progress slowly through the afternoon. Frequently you stop on some high point, dismount and listen while your foreman points there and there and there, discussing the range. He mentions that some of your forest land could be logged for lumber. Half a dozen times he points out fresh tracks and droppings from deer, and once you come on a partially-eaten carcass of a yearling calf.

"Painter," your foreman states. "I'll haf to send a man up here."

You say nothing. Maybe it's a month before you learn, accidentally, that a "painter" is really a panther, and that panther **is** another name for the big sleek mountain lion of the West which kills many calves, colts, deer, goats, sheep, even grown horses on occasion.

"I'll just mark the trail," your man says now. He selects a prominent rock, a boulder the size of a sedan. On top of this he puts another rock as big as his hat, and on top of that a rock like a cocoanut. (Weeks later you deduce that those stacked rocks, visible for a long way up the canyon, were to guide the hunter and hound, who were sent up that way to pick up the panther's trail, tree it somewhere, and kill it. You figure that out when the foreman brings you in the panther's beautiful tan pelt one day as a trophy, which you blushingly accept even though you didn't do the actual killing.)

By now, however, you are quite tired, and your dainty gold wrist watch informs you that the hour is after 4 P.M.

All at once you realize that you could not possibly find your way back home, back to the ranch house. Why, you have been riding for hours, in climbs and twists and circles, up a maze of canyons, in thick brush and in rocky forests! Looking back now, you see nothing familiar at all. Worry consumes you.

"It'll be colder up here, but not *so* cold," your man declares presently. "Reckon you planned to lay out, all right?"

"Er, I beg pardon?" You stare vacantly at him.

"Yes, sir," he pretends to think you spoke in agreement, and so guides your horse with his. "We can manage to keep warm. Plenty of wood up here."

You swallow, and ride on. There are quite a few knee-high rocks up here on this table land, but you observe a lot of dry grass between them, and realize it would be green grass in spring. You don't find many cows. You deduce (rather proudly) that they have gone to the lower altitudes for the winter months, and your foreman verifies that opinion when you mention it. Thinking on, you realize that the lower deserts will be dried up in summer, and then this upland will be the place for your stock to live. By now something of the magnitude of your ranch has begun to dawn on you. You are fatigued, but proud. Happy, even.

"Good a spot as any, I reckon," your man decides, stopping beside a cliff and dismounting. It has become almost dark now. Quickly, deftly, he unsaddles both horses and hobbles them so they can eat but not stray far away. Your man produces an unexpected canteen of water, shares it with you. As you drink, he stirs up a little fire about eight feet from the cliff wall. Presently he has brought in armloads of dried wood and the fire is bigger. You go to help him, breaking off limbs

of scrub oak trees, mountain laurel, anything that has chanced
to die and dry. You carry in quite a pile, then stand around
looking at the blaze. The stack of wood looks like a big reserve,
to you.

"Might as well eat what's left," your foreman suggests, and
the two of you devour the remaining cold biscuits and beef.
It is not enough, but it takes the sting of hunger away. You
talk a little more freely now. Both of you feel pretty good,
sitting here with your backs to the cliff, looking at the fire.
The thought occurs to you that this is highly picturesque,
theatrical. Over a ridge yonder you can look far down into
the low valley—your ranch includes this spectacular physio-
graphic rim. Here the dancing light plays on the cliff nearer
at hand, and on the boulders scattered in the distance. You
conjure up thoughts of wild animals, but dismiss them. Before
eight o'clock, your face is stretched in a prodigious yawn, in
spite of the rather pleasant conversation.

"Me too," your friend (he has become that) says, at this
juncture. "It's late anyhow."

Late! Before 8 P.M.!

But you do not protest when he carries both saddles to a spot
between the fire and the wall, and gives you your saddle
blanket.

Watching him, you inspect yours to discover it is a thick,
good grade of wool. If it smells horsy, no matter. The foreman thoughtfully spread it a while ago so that any sweat
dampness could dry in this thin Arizona mountain air. Now
he calmly rolls up in his blanket, puts his head on his saddle
and his hat over his face, and says "Good-night." You roll
up and lie down on the good firm earth beside him—nursing
the strangest thoughts in all your career!

By dawn you have learned some more things:

That the fire was reflected onto you by the nearby cliff, to keep both "beds" surprisingly warm. That your foreman must have replenished the fire several times, for the wood is low. That you, who expected not to sleep a wink, knew nothing for almost nine consecutive hours. That you can get up—although stiffly—before 5 A.M. and actually like it.

Up here, a faint glow of daylight is showing at this hour. The deep canyon at your ranch house delayed the light of dawn down there. You think forcefully of breakfast. Will your man work another miracle?

He will not!

He and you both saddle and ride again, on refreshed horses, just as it gets light enough to see the land clearly. Sundry birds and other small unseen animals are startled by you, but mostly you are concerned with keeping your ears and hands warm.

"Cuppa hot coffee'd go good," your friend suggests.

You grin acknowledgment, but nothing else is said about it.

Nor is anything done. To your discomfort as well as surprise, you ride all morning without a bite to eat or drink. You find the "upper eight hundred," discover it is eight hundred acres of especially good range. It is quite high, and covered under a foot of snow. A lot more snow is stacked in the rocks beyond it. That means, your foreman says happily, that the acreage will be well watered this spring, and will give the cattle there a fine start. He will have his men drive up a select herd of yearlings. They'll fatten good, and bring a top price.

You tighten your belt and ride on. Presently you note that you are riding down hill again, slowly but surely. You also see that the hour is 10 A.M. And you haven't the slightest idea where you are, or how to find your way back to any human habitation. For twenty-four hours you have been in a region as wild as it was two centuries ago.

You are coming down a warm southern slope, rather rocky, when all at once your foreman stops his horse, unholsters his six-shooter and cracks down—BANG!

"Br-r-r-rr-r-r-r!" A sudden rattling, as of dried peas in a dried pod. Yonder on a rock bathed in sunshine.

"Little early for rattlesnakes," says your man. "But I reckon he was brought out by this February sun."

You are astounded by it all. One bullet had neatly clipped the reptile's neck, almost severing the body from the head. The marksman casually cuts off the rattles—nine of them— with his pocket knife, presents them to you, meanwhile talking about something else entirely.

By 1:30 P.M. you feel that you have ridden over most of the United States and Canada, when suddenly you top a rise and lo—there in the middle distance is the place from which you started! Yonder, in an unexpected direction, lies your ranch home!

Your horses know it too. They perk up noticeably. Your foreman hangs one knee over his saddle horn, the better to face you as you ride. He feels better. He has decided, slowly, that you are a pretty good fellow, doggone it. You didn't know much, but you were a good sport. You never complained. You "took" it. Now if he can just get you to let him alone, he will make your ranch pay. He is glad he can like you, as a man. In time, a long time, he'll educate you, and everything will be hunky-dory. All of this you begin to sense, as his conversation waxes a bit more personal, even a trifle intimate and jocular. If you are smart at all you will realize you have been slowly creating a precious new friendship these past thirty-three hours.

When you finally do get home, get a drink of water, get an inconceivable amount of grub inside your stomach again, you also realize something of the magnitude of your ranch. You begin to have some conception of its ruggedness, of its problems.

And you can begin to understand what conditions prevail at branding time.

CHAPTER II

TWO FIRES

In GENERAL, there are two circumstances under which cattle get branded. First is the day-by-day routine of the ranch.

A regulation cowboy, earning his $40 a month and keep, will normally be going about the expansive ranch on any one of a hundred duties, and will be carrying a branding iron on his saddle to label such new calves and unmarked old stock as he happens to encounter. He may ride with another cowboy for cooperative work and company, or he may ride alone.

In our hypothesis, therefore, imagine yourself this time to be not the new ranch owner and boss but one of the hands. Imagine you are sixty miles from the nearest railroad, twenty miles from an automobile road, and ten miles from any human habitation. Away yonder to your left is Tonto Mountain, and clouds have slipped playfully down its side so that the actual cone-top seems cut off and floating mistily in space. To your right, still farther away, are Four Peaks, landmarks so dominant that in Phoenix a lot of things, including beer and butter, are named for them; but you know they are eighty miles from you, however intrusive they appear. You are riding along a fairly smooth valley between lesser red-and-blue mountains, and because you are lonesome you may be singing, even though without benefit of guitar, spotlight or microphone.

15

"Ay, ay, ay-ay,
Canta y no llores,
Porque cantando se alegran
Cielito lindo los corazones."

You'll be singing in Spanish because you are typical; an Arizona or other border-state cowboy associates with greasers [1]
so much that he is likely to speak a hybrid language even when cussing or praying (if he ever gets around to doing any of the latter).

All at once, however, you jump a yearling bull. Maybe it was your singing, or your horse, or both, that frightened him. No matter. There he is in the thorny brush, a bucky young fellow with his tail up and his head down. He is unquestionably wild and frightened and not a little ferocious. You who are a cowboy must tie into him, knowing that an accident might cost your life.

But you do not hesitate. In a few seconds your lariat rope is free and you are twirling a loop. You spur your horse, who is smart enough to need no further command or direction. Putt-a-putt, putt-a-putt, putt-a-putt—swish-swish—throw!

The loop snakes out with incredible speed and accuracy. You have snubbed your end of the rope around your saddle horn. Your horse stiff-legs to a halt. The bull, who has just seen his first human and is having the surprise of his young life, somersaults grandly, with a thump and groan.

You quickly dismount and tie the bull's four feet together with your piggin' string (short rope), leaving the horse to keep the lariat tight, then you gather a handful of twigs, dry grass, cow chips, or whatever is near you that will burn. You build a fire. You poke your branding iron into it. When it begins to

[1] That is, Mexicans. The terms are synonymous, to cowboys.

show pinkish red (maybe you shield the sunlight from it with your hat, to see its heat color) you know it is ready for use.

If you are skillful and intend to do nothing but brand, you may be able to dab on the hot iron without further tying of the animal. It depends on many little details—whether the bull is being docile, whether it is standing, or down. Sometimes you can brand and be gone before the bull can lunge away. More often you have to tie its feet together and use your strong left arm to hold them while you apply the iron with the right. Remember, too, that meanwhile you are sweating under a scorching mid-August sun; or freezing under a mid-January blizzard. For you are fighting the weather as much as you are fighting isolation and its dangers, in addition to the bull.

In any event the crucial moment comes quickly. You run from the fire, slap down the iron—*S-s-s-s-s-s-!* "BAW-W-W-W!" The hair burns, live flesh fries. There is an acrid odor, strong, repulsive; no man ever likes it.

You drop the iron. You take out your pocket knife, operate, then move from the bull's rump to his head. Deftly you slit a design in one or both ears, actually cutting out pieces of the ear and throwing them away. (Ear-marking, while a common adjunct of branding, is not used on all ranches.) By this time the smell of blood has been added to that of burning flesh and hair, and your hands are red and gory. Once in a great while you might—just might—pause at this point for a moment to wonder where is the alleged romance in ranching. More likely, though, you'd get blood slung in your eyes and get a hoof kick in your stomach if you paused for any sort of meditation. So, you just slip off the lariat loop and jump back as fast as you can.

You re-coil your rope and tie it to your saddle. Your horse appears to be dozing, bored with it all. The branded steer runs off, perhaps still rumbling. (Since it was a bull, remember you will also have castrated.) You wipe your bloody hands on grass and leaves. Then again you take up your iron. It is still hot, so you wave it in the air, dig it into damp earth if any is available. Pretty soon you can tie it back on the saddle and ride on.

Perhaps you were out on a special branding mission. More likely the branding was incidental to some other mission such as inspection for range feed, for water, fence damage, diseases, rustlers. If on this foray you have a human companion you are lucky indeed, but in any event your day's work is cut out for you. Down the arroyo a way will be other unbranded stock, so that over and over your little action-drama must be repeated.

In the movies you have seen the handsome hero dash out and lasso one cow, sashay around in the muck and dirt, and appear in the very next close-up clean and spick and span enough to kiss the heroine. Well, friend, only a mother would kiss you after you have branded and ear-marked and castrated a few real range bulls, and you can rest assured that your pink silk bandanna and your white stetson would be nasty as sin. But we're forgetting our hypothesis: you wouldn't be wearing pink and white in the first place. Pink and white aren't going to have much place in your life after you move to the rancho; black and brown are going to make up your personal color scheme.

On another day and under much more social conditions, though, you will be on a different branding spree. This will be the ranch roundup time.

Now a great deal has already been written about the roundup, and a whole book could be written here, for it is grand he-pageantry, important and interesting and American to the core. The roundup may be any day of the year and may be big or little. That is, the ranch-owner may have occasion to gather in a part of a herd at any time, and so do the necessary branding. But in general the main roundups are in the fall and the spring, to inspect the stock, take out those to be sold, count the increase, brand the new calves and the ones that escaped branding last year, cut out animals from other ranch herds, castrate bulls, doctor them for blackleg or other diseases, make sales to buyers who may be on hand, and incidentally have such fun as the hard work will permit. A big ranch will have a big roundup, sometimes with neighboring ranches sending their cowboys to help. Then the assembly point becomes a show place indeed—a spectacular, highly picturesque movie set, without the cameras. The herd may number into the thousands, and include cows of several owners. Then by brands and ear-marks alone can ownership be determined. (Ear-marks help identify in the dust and rush, but they are just supplementary to the larger, more important brands.)

Since you are one of the riders in the group handling the herd that day, you will have hard work to do, but you will enjoy high sociability. Your first work will be reading the marks and brands. You must have a quick eye, a quick memory, a knowledge of many brands—not just your own. (The word "brand" is often used inclusively, referring to all marks of identification, including the burned monogram and the ear-slits if the latter are employed.)

The branding work is not done single-handed here, but in rapid cooperation. One big fire is built, so that a great bed of glowing coals is available. Long-handled irons, maybe six or a dozen or more, are stuck there to heat. Two men are squatting near, ready. Out of the big milling, bawling herd two hundred yards or so away will come a high-tailed calf, running with a rope around its neck and with you the cowboy hazing it on.

"Lazy Y Bar!" you will shout as you rein your horse.

Plop! Over tumbles the calf, somersaulted by the sudden stop, momentarily stunned. Two strong men grab its legs and stretch it, on its side. The horse is keeping the neck rope tight. A man has come running from the fire.

S-s-s-s-s-s and the acrid smell again, a quick ear-cut, the bawl of pain. The rope is slipped off. The calf is shunted into the Lazy Y Bar herd half-a-mile down the hill.

"Box S!"

Another shout. Another cowboy has come out of the herd with a calf, and another man has come running with a different iron. The branding process is being repeated before a dude guest can quite realize it. Indeed, the men had better hurry, for yonder comes a third calf, and behind that still a fourth! It may keep up for hours. And two or three groups may be so working.

The mounted men will have determined ownership of the calves by watching what mothers they follow. A calf clinging near a mother branded $\boxed{\text{S}}$ is obviously a Box S calf, for even though all cows look much alike to men, they have individualities to each other. No calf ever mistakes its mother, if she is near (although in hunger it will nurse another), and no mother ever mistakes her calf. Looking at it from the bovine viewpoint, don't you imagine human beings all look much alike to cows, and that the cows conceivably wonder how we identify each other? That's one of nature's secrets. Maybe it's looks, or smell, or vibrations, or all three.

In the big general herd will be quite a few grown animals with no brands. Some will be masculine, some feminine; all will be valuable. If five ranches have cooperated on the roundup, whose animals are these?

The matter is determined by selling all these mavericks to the highest bidder, or by equal division, or by any means to which the owners may agree. When it is settled, the appropriate brands are put on as before.

A variation of this roundup system is that of employing a chute whereby cows are pushed into a pen, squeezed into momentary helplessness, and branded while standing. The chute method is not nearly so spectacular but is used to advantage under certain conditions. (Detailed discussion is given chute branding in Chapter VI, "Tools and Techniques.")

In the case of all the animals branded, supplementary treatment often includes not only castration of bulls, but hypodermic "shots" as required. Injection of serum to prevent the disease called blackleg is usually done at this time. And as in the matter of castration, the movies and the story writers almost never mention blackleg shots, just as they never mention screw worms, nor wolf worms, nor scabies, ticks, lumpy jaw, tuberculosis, anthrax, or teat fever. These things, it appears, are not romantic. Nor picturesque.

You will hear, too, that branding is extreme and unnecessary cruelty. But you will realize that a brand is not an ugly scar burned on an animal just for the deviltry of it. Ranchers are no more cruel than butchers or bankers or politicians. It is a distinct pleasure and privilege to associate with ranchers, for among them are no jitterbugs, gigolos, neurotics, or weaklings, even though there is a normal quantity of dishonesty and mean-ness. Perhaps the finest sentiments and the finest imaginations lurk not in the world's artists and scholars, but in the strong men who glory in the more dangerous labor required of human-ity. Have you not observed it, for added instance, in men of the sea? There is, then, a deep something in ranch folk which transcends all such trivia as fatigue and loneliness and bloody hands.

This becomes apparent when we examine not the painful act of branding, but the stories back of the brand designs.

CHAPTER III

SINCE 2000 B.C.

WHEN you, the new ranch owner of Chapter I, came back from that first long ride of inspection, you decided forthwith that it was necessary to create a ranch brand of your own. Probably you got around to considering it that very night in front of your big living-room fireplace.

You have spread paper and pencils over the massive hand-hewn table there, and you and your wife and maybe your hypothetical grown-up son and daughter are present. You have all come from the cold Northeast of cities and sin, to the storied space and goodness of cowboyland. You were a Success back there in business and finance, and having earned your money you came to retire on a ranch before you got too old and lost your enthusiasms. You like this ranching idea more and more. You feel that you actually need your own brand.

"Alicia studied art at Vassar," mother suggests. "Let her design it."

But you snort in masculine contempt. You should say not! This is a he-man ranch, your ranch, with rocks and mountains and—and manure and everything on it. You spit defiantly into the fireplace and take up the pencil yourself.

Now your name, let us say, is Jim Kirby, a good average American name. Since you made it a success in business, you feel that it ought not to be ignored now. You sketch tentatively—let's see, Jim Kirby, Jim Kirby, unh-huhm . . . J

. . . J . . . J-K, Jim Kirby, J-K . . . yes, sir, that's it! You combine the J and the K and all at once you have a masterpiece:

$$\cancel{K}$$

"Look a-here," you call, proudly.

It looks like a cattle brand, sure enough. See how the J and the K unite their main stems? Wouldn't that look fine on cow hides, heh-heh?

You think it is mighty clever, but it isn't. Making your brand this way is really a form of ego. You should have kept the truly beautiful old Two Hearts brand which your cows now wear, thereby showing your sentimental respect for a highly sentimental past. But you aren't that broadminded and, being hypothetically typical, you go ahead and make your brand out of your initials just as many thousands of other ranchers have done. Experimentally you heat the poker in the fireplace and burn the JK design on a kindling board. It looks pretty good. It looks like a cattle brand.

That's what you wanted. Of course you realize that all your stock can't magically change from Two Hearts to JK over night. The change will take a year or two. Next morning you show the sketch to your foreman, who just signifies by his manner that you are the boss.

"A heap of people will be right sorry to see the old Two Hearts pass on," he remarks, neither of you realizing that he is pronouncing an obituary. You have killed something and don't know it. By 1960 nobody will remember anything at all about the young Tormeys who pioneered your ranch from the elements and the Indians.

The foreman says it's a good enough brand, and do you want him to register it? You hadn't known about that; but the fact is, cattle brands have to be registered much as any other trademark. And your brand *is* your trademark, in rangeland; in time you can build on it, making it known and respected and valuable. You or your agent will have to make formal application to the Livestock Sanitary Board in Phoenix, or to some similar governmental body in any other state, writing your desire to register the brand you have drawn.

Under Arizona law, your notice is duly advertised by the Board in certain specified publications likely to be seen by other ranch men. The public has a limited time in which to file protest against your brand. Maybe your JK is exactly like John Knight's over in Mohave County, and so yours will be denied. Or maybe the Board, inspecting yours, will decide that it could be altered too easily by rustlers, or that you could burn yours too easily over a simpler brand already registered and so be a rustler yourself. In either case you would then be notified and you would have to choose another brand. Some states, notably Texas, have held to county rather than state registration of brands; hence considerable duplication has resulted. But it has done little harm because of the great distances between counties there. El Paso and Harris, for instance, both great cattle counties in Texas, are still two days apart even by fast automobile travel.

Assuming, though, that your JK is passed and registered, it is henceforth the property of you or your heirs or assigns, and no other person in your state may use it, under penalty of law. It is now truly your trademark, your copyright. If you catch a man putting the JK brand on any sort of animal hereafter, you can ride right up and claim the animal for your own, even though it is a prize $2,000 bull belonging to some town dairy. And if you catch some man messing around with your branded cows, trying to alter your brand in any way, you can shoot him through the shoulder, drag him into court, hear the judge say you have technically violated a law by shooting, but hear a jury of your fellow-ranchers ask you why in the devil you had such a poor aim.

When you have learned all of this from your foreman, your pride in your self-created brand increases. The old JK begins to take on significance right away. You learn somewhere that western ranches are seldom referred to by name. A cowboy, asking you for a job, doesn't recommend himself by saying, "I worked ten years for Mr. Cal Noble in Cochise County, and you can ask him about me." He says: "I punched fer ten year on the old X Bar A down in Cock-eyes, yais sir." He figures that if you don't know who owns the X Bar A, and don't understand what Cock-eyes [1] is, he doesn't want to work for you anyway. Moreover, the fact that he could stick ten years on one job is ample recommendation, without inviting you to ask his former boss for a testimonial. If you're smart, you'll hire the man.

Increasingly through that month and year, indeed through all the remainder of your life, you'll find the JK trademark clinging to you. The chances are you'll come to love it, and so stamp it on your saddles, gates, barns, jewelry, letterheads and such, as we shall see. It becomes a very personal thing to you and your family and those loyal ones whom you employ, because of the work, worry, trouble and triumph—the general living—which will surely be associated with it as the years go by.

As you gradually discover that fact, you will also deduce the answer to a question which will have popped into your mind,

[1] Correct pronunciation of this southern Arizona county is "co-cheés." But of course the boys have to have their fun with it.

as it often pops into a business man's mind: "Why aren't brands made simply as numbers, much as automobiles are registered? Wouldn't it be more efficient?"

Yes. Yes, surely. By various combinations of initials and numbers, every cow in Christendom could be branded in different fashion from every other cow; hence it would be quite simple to give every ranch an individual number. A small pocket notebook could carry the 1940 ranch registrations, let us say, for quick reference. It would be very businesslike, efficient, modern, American, and all that.

But for the Lord's sake let's retain *something* of beauty in our modern living, gentlemen! Something of the heritage our fathers left. It's a trifle harder to memorize a lot of jumbled curlicues burned on a cow's rump, but it's a lot more fun. What if we could make a hundred dollars a year more money by being a trifle more efficient in branding? We aren't in such a gosh-awful dither to make money out on the range. We like it out here, where seldom is heard a discouraging word and the deer and the antelope—and the people—play.

Nobody today knows just when or where branding originated.

Within the past year a reputable newspaper in a cattle state printed a two-column headline saying, FIRST CATTLE BRANDS WERE USED ON XIT RANCH, which was so stupid as to be inexcusable; the XIT ranch is but yesterday's child, even though it does not exist today. A radio "educator" recently stated that branding originated on the ranch of a Spanish pioneer in Texas, and another radio orator said that branding was exclusively an American process "necessary at the outset but so crude and cruel as to be practically obsolete now."

Bosh! It is neither Spanish, Texan, American, crude, cruel, obsolete, nor even obsolescent.

The Oriental Institute of the University of Chicago probably is the best authority in this field, by virtue of long research, but it is not the only one that can prove that branding was done at least two thousand years before Christ. Tombs in Egypt not only show the ancient brands, but picture the actual work of branding; and, except that the costume of the cowboys is quite different, the scene might just as well be in Texas or Wyoming or Montana or California or Idaho. Mostly the name or sign of some god seems to have been chosen for the brand, but not always. Sometimes there was a temple brand. One pictured ox has a brand on its rump showing that it belonged to Herd Number 43.

Elsewhere in this book we explain how the early Egyptians, Romans, Greeks, and others fire-branded criminals and slaves. During the same periods, branding of livestock was common practice. There is biblical evidence that Jacob the great herdsman branded his stock. Chinese ideographs have been branded on animals so long that probably not even Confucius could have said when the practice started. The crossed hammers of Solingen was burned on animals and stamped on swords in the Middle Ages. The Broad Arrowhead (British Imperial Brand) was burned on animals, burned into the butts of lances, and then on rifles and other equipment from about the time of the Battle of Crécy on.

Hernando Cortez doubtless brought the first branding irons to the New World. He needn't have bothered, really, because there were no other cattle or horses on this continent to mingle with his for quite a while, but the hardy Spaniard believed in preparedness. He expected to travel and fight a lot, and did so; he wouldn't have had time to mine, smelt and work American-born metal into a stamping iron. In 1540 Coronado came northward on the greatest treasure hunt in American history, entered what is now Arizona, and roamed about the Southwest for two years; he had branded cattle with him. That was four hundred years ago. It wasn't very long as time goes, however, before other Spaniards over here owned competitive herds, and of course the redoubtable Yankee came onto the scene pretty soon.

With the coming of the Yankee practical necessity called for brands, and so brands were used. The peculiar circumstances in his nation, however, foreordained the biggest and altogether greatest cattle enterprise in the history of the world, created a new man—the cowboy—and lifted branding from a mere tagging to a boast of heraldry.

Thus does pre-history, history, tradition, everything, prove that you are entering a select society when you desert the cities, design your own brand, and join the hosts of cattle kings.

CHAPTER IV

AMERICAN PYROGLYPHICS

Suppose somebody told you that the Rocking M, the Chain Seven, the Saddle Pockets, the Two Lazy Two P, the Pig Pen, the Mashed Oh, the Dog Iron, and the Associated Press were all going to assemble next March in Skeleton Canyon to bull-dog and auger. If you lived on the Llano Estacado of Texas or in the hills of Wyoming you would simply nod and say thanks, I'll shore be there. But if you were an average Easterner you would have to ask a lot of questions. Not even the encyclo-pedias could help you.

A restaurant in Midland, Texas, every few days paints a big sign on its window:

MOUNTAIN OYSTERS
FRESH TODAY

The advertisement, which draws good trade, is not aimed primarily at tourists, although many a tourist orders the oysters in blind faith.

The U.S. Postmen once correctly delivered a letter, mailed in New York, addressed only:

I O I

If Professor Throckmorton Q. Abercrombie, Ph.D., of Har-vard and Oxford, happened to be around an Arizona chuck-wagon at supper time, he might in a moment of sociability remark that "the transcendentalism of Kant tends to affirm the existence of *a priori* principles of cognition."

30

"Yes, suh, thet's a fack," the cowboy on his left would acknowledge, politely, but he wouldn't know what the hell the professor was talking about.

"It was a Hashknife paint and two mavericks got in th' Forked S remuda today," the cowboy would say, presently—and then the professor wouldn't know what the hell.

In short, there is a nomenclature of the range, especially a brand alphabet and language, which is as intriguing as Sanskrit and almost as hard to learn unless you are brought up with it. The cowboy can be forgiven, because he hasn't had the opportunity to study book philosophy; but the broadly literate Dr. Abercrombies have persistently ignored the Americana of cowboyland.

Of course the most fascinating phase of the study is in the motives and meanings back of cattle brands, the stories they tell, rather than in the mere naming of them and their parts, and this will be given due attention later. But it is essential that we learn something of how to pronounce and read these range pyroglyphics before we set out to translate them.

In learning any foreign language we begin with the short easy words and translations. Brands are read from top to bottom and from left to right. The brand alphabet begins with plane geometry in its simplest form. First is the ordinary line, a short line, which may run crossways, up and down, or at an angle. With each change of position it acquires a new name.

A long straight horizontal line like this ▬▬ is a *rail*. Obviously, it looks like a rail, such as ranchers use on their corral fences. Two of them are called *two rails:* ▬▬. But, remarkably, when three of them are used they cease to suggest rails to the cowboy, so he has named them *stripes:* ▬▬▬.

However, don't feel too smug about learning that Number One fact, because if the rail is shortened a trifle it ceases to be a rail and becomes a *bar*. Come to think of it, a bar might be used on that same corral fence, and sure enough it would be a shorter piece of timber. But the precise difference in length, as used in brands, is likely to confuse the uninitiated. Roughly, the rail is burned about six to eight inches long, and the bar three or four. If the brander gets careless and lets his bar run too long, he ought to be ashamed of himself in the first place, and he and his buddies have to remember it in the second place. Arguments and fist fights have resulted about just such trivia as an inch on a burned line.

Now the rail is almost never turned straight up, perpendicular, for the excellent reason that it is very difficult to brand it that way on a cow's rough contours. But it frequently is turned up at an angle like this: \ or this / in which case it acquires a new name, *slash*. It is relatively easy to burn the shorter bar as a perpendicular line, but it may lose its identity then, and become just what it looks like, the letter I or the numeral 1.

O is called what it appears to be, a *circle*. Usually it is distinguished from the letter O by being larger and more nearly round, but a small round circle may be called O if combined with other letters or numerals. If the circle is squashed down a little horizontally it becomes aptly named a *mashed O* or a *goose egg:* ◯. The *half circle* and the *quarter circle* are commonly used also, and are called by those names; but if either of these segments happens to be part of a drawn brand it may lose its identity. Thus ⋃ is the *Quarter Circle U* brand, but ⋒ is the *Swinging H*. Wherever the circle segment resembles a chair rocker, the brand is likely to be named *rocking;* thus the *Rocking R* ℞. Carrying that descriptive idea still further, this well-known brand is called the *Rocking Chair* ⊔ .

The straight line and the circle are the bases, and from this point on, the alphabet of branding is a logical and altogether ingenious adaptation of plane geometry, the English alphabet, and the Arabic numerals. Your cleverness can have full freedom when you go to design a brand; your imagination or lack of it will be stamped as permanently on your reputation as it is on your cows. In reading brands as well as in creating them, a study of the following progression will help:

This is one of innumerable uses of the rail, here to make the *T Rail T* brand. It might have been reversed to make it *Rail T Rail.*

Here the form of the rail is retained but the name lost. This combination of four rails is known as the *Pigpen* brand. Every cow state has a Pigpen brand; sometimes it is made of six rails crossed, or even eight and ten. Obviously crosses, squares, diamonds and triangles could evolve from this too.

And here appears not only an initial D, but another adaptation of the straight lines. This brand is read *D Bench.*

In Nevada this one is called the *Half Box H Half Box.* More poetic Arizonians using the same brand called it the *Flying H.* (But "flying" ordinarily has a slightly different connotation. See below, page 36.)

The *Bar* is perhaps the best known brand term. A great many dudes think that all brands must, by some vague law, have a bar in them, but as a matter of fact the bar is not an especially good brand part because it invites "strikeover" or re-designing by rustlers. The word "bar" is used in a great many brand names in fiction and songs. The K L Bar, the Bar B Q, the Bar J are a few typical bar brands. The *M Bar V* is pictured here; it is the brand of a famous ranch (now herding dudes) near Wickenburg, Arizona, where for years cowboys have been singing "I'll love her and she'll love me, at roundup time on the M Bar V."

Many other uses of the bar of course suggest themselves. For instance, the teacher and the school pupil will immediately envision brands called plus and minus. In range language, however, these old symbols are called Cross and Bar. The sign for division in arithmetic is called Dot Bar Dot on the range. One of the most famous of the relatively simple straight line designs of this sort, but without the "bar" name, was developed on the beautiful Tod ranch in New Mexico. The brand and its importance are preserved today by Jim Tod of Phoenix, Arizona, formerly of Maple Hill, Kansas. It is called the *Cross L*, and is made by burning a straight bar across the long stem of the capital letter L.

A square or rectangle in cow language becomes box or block. Diamonds and triangles identify themselves. When a half diamond is made, opening downward, the cowboy may call it that, or he may call it a Rafter because it suggests the gable of a house. In the latter instance the angle formed is obtuse, usually. A smaller or acute angle is called just what it appears to be—*Open A* (that is to say, an A without the horizontal bar).

HEL This one from Culberson County, Texas, is the *Hell Bar*, although stretching the bar under three initials makes it technically a rail. Thus do we get into what might be termed the idiom of brand language!

Where there aren't many competitive brands or much danger from rustlers the plain *Circle* may be found; simplicity in brand design is always of practical value. The Hipolito Garcia ranch on the Nueces River in Southwest Texas, famous in the late 1800's, used a plain broad circle. Circles can be combined or grouped almost endlessly. These two are called the *Lapped Circles* brand.

And these are the *Three Links*. Obviously Four Links, Five Links, or more, might be used in such a chain brand.

If the circles are not touching, they might or might not be called circles. This brand, for instance, is referred to as the *Double Oh*. The Triple Oh and the Four Ohs are known also. But if some rancher called them circles, or rings, or zeros, he'd still be right. The rules are flexible, and the readings vary from county to county, state to state, not only in the case of circles but with many other designs as well. Thus the brand language becomes as polyglot as Chinese.

All those above are relatively simple brand specimens, typical of hundreds of thousands that have been registered, or just used, since animals were first domesticated. They are important as elementary studies in cowrography, but they reveal little of beauty and ingenuity, novelty and humor. Consider, however, the few typical exhibits that follow, and the exquisite picture language of them.

The simple straight-line initial Y often has been used as a brand in itself, but a touch of comedy and originality was added by the fellow who made his the *Walking Y*. By the simple process of putting legs and feet on them, other letters, numerals, and objects frequently are made to walk.

If the brand is to "run", however, the technique is different. An initial does not run on legs; it runs simply by extending itself as if it were in one gosh-awful hurry, and by leaning slightly ahead. Here is a *Running M*.

The cowboys of past centuries observed and envied the birds, so that brands have been flying for a long, long time. All anything needs to fly with is wings, of course. Older readers may recall a book of popular fiction called "Chip of the *Flying U*". Here's Chip's brand.

Literally thousands of brands have been designed by ranchers sketching objects near at hand. His hat perhaps is the item of dress in which a cowman takes most pride, and this is reflected in numerous *Hat* brands, of which three versions are pictured here.

Among objects, a cowman's saddle comes next in his affections, and so the various parts of a saddle are found in extensive use in brand designing. Here for example is one form of the *Stirrup* brand. Bridle bits, spurs, saddle bags, saddle horn, all have been used.

Nature and the elements had a profound influence on the success or failure of a ranching enterprise, and on the ranchmen. Half moons, new moons, sunsets and sunrises (made very much alike—a half circle with light rays going up spokewise), rainfall, clouds, all are common brand designs. Most impressive of nature's spectacles of course is the thunderstorm, so the *Forked Lightning* brand, shown here, grew from that.

In the old days ranchers were likely to spend a great deal of time fighting or worrying about Indians, and this memory is handed down to us moderns in the *Broken Arrow* brand. You can readily imagine, too, the brand adaptations of the tomahawk, arrowhead (thousands of 'em), feathered headdress, and other Indian symbols.

Incidentally, the Indians themselves seldom
bothered to do any branding, and even then did
it more for "art" or through religious-decorative
motives than as a means of identification.

Still other common objects sure to be impressed on the rancher's mind, and from which
he might draw the inspiration for his brand, were
wild animals, large and small. There are mountain lion brands, wildcat brands, bighorn brands,
innumerable snake brands, of course, Gila mon-
ster brands, armadillo brands, buzzard brands,
squirrel brands, and so on ad infinitum. Here-
with is a simple and rather cute one, the *Baby
Turtle* brand.

But what of the objects in vegetable nature?
Did they not impress the rancher too? Surely!
The registries have a great many tree brands,
some of which are very clever adaptations. There
is inevitably a Christmas tree brand, an oak leaf,
a windblown tree (all limbs blown to the left),
and a sort of futuristic or cubistic tree brand.
There seems to be infinite variation in the actual
design itself, but the *Tree* brand is most often
called by just that name.

It is easy to understand how a man just starting in the cow business would sit down at night,
when he had a moment to relax around the supper fire, and there design the brand he wanted
to register. The influence of such a moment is

revealed in thousands of brands built of axes, buckets, pots, forks, spoons, skillets. The most famous and best loved cowboy who ever lived had an andiron design for a brand. (See page 137.) The typical one here is a *Camp Kettle* brand.

Or of course the extremely busy young rancher might have finished building his first little shack just before he found time to design a brand for his new herd, and then, proud of his carpentry, immortalized it. Here is a typical *House* brand.

Maybe he married sweet Susie in town and they had a baby before they moved into the little ranch house, and the baby girl had a doll, and the man discovered that he simply had to create a brand for his new-born calves. The baby put her doll in daddy's lap after supper one night, and lo—the *Dollbaby* brand. At least that's one known instance of how it happened. But there are many dollbaby brands. (The story of another one is told in a famous range legend.)

You'll note that we have graduated into sentiment now. From rails and bars, circles and initials, through objects into symbolism which knows no end. Westerners know that the young John Tormeys in Arizona used a Two Hearts brand, as a monument to their married love. Well, all manner of hearts have been used in designing brands: single hearts, double hearts,

triple hearts, hearts interlocked, hearts punctured by Cupid's arrows, fat hearts, long slender
hearts, all kinds. Here is pictured one which
must have a poignant story behind it. You can
guess its name.

We have already indicated that the most common cattle brands are those based on initials,
either single, double or triple. Millions of them
have been used, with many duplications, and
whatever they may have lacked in originality
they probably made up in satisfactory service.
First grouping here naturally is the plain initials,
such as any man nowadays might ink on his golf
bag and his gym shoes and die-stamp on his expensive carpenter tools, and such as his wife
might embroider on his handkerchiefs and pillow slips. They serve for identification. They
titillate the ego satisfactorily. But they are evidence of "practical" minds rather than imaginative ones, and it is significant that their plainness
has been avoided so many times. You can read
and translate them only one way—literally. This
typical one is simply the *J H D* brand as registered by crusty old John Henry Doe.

Of course John Henry could have done much
better if he hadn't been such an emphatically
practical old cuss. He could have added just this
little fillip of distinction to his brand, in which
case it would have been named the *J H D Connected*. The common *A P Connected*, with their

main stems joined as one, is often referred to as the *Associated Press* brand since that news association began branding all its news items with the linotype. Ranch folk have labored to give their initial brands "looks". They may have leaned backward over it at times, but they have had their fun, and so have we who study them.

Sometimes not the three initials of a name but the given name or nickname of the rancher or his wife is woven into the brand design. Many a Robert somebody, nicknamed Bob, has taken out his pencil and notebook, or has begun scratching in the sand, to evolve this version of the *B O B* brand. It is usually pronounced as three letters, not as "Bob".

Yet another series of groupings are those made of Arabic numerals. Doubtless the most famous of all these is the Hundred and One Ranch brand from Oklahoma, which is given detailed treatment in many writings. But a survey of the brand registries will show countless brands made up simply of one, two, three, four and (rarely) five or six numerals. Often they have some private significance (as in the notorious case of the 6666, also related in detail by range biographers) but apparently most of them were originated solely in answer to an immediate need of a "tag" or identifying trademark. Threes, sevens and nines seem to dominate, if we ignore the zero which doubles as an "Oh" and a "Circle". This representative example is called just what it shouts—*Ninety-nine*.

Frequently the imagery and beauty is heightened, just as in the case of the letter combinations, by joining the numerals together. The strokes of several pairs seem to invite making Siamese twins of them, so to speak. The *Seventy-Six* or *Seven Six* brand here pictured is a very common one, found in every state and in foreign lands as well. The perpendicular short stroke of a 5 frequently becomes also the perpendicular cross stroke of a 4. The back and base of a 2 can become the front and cross line of a 4. And there are others.

Next consideration is the combination of initials and numbers, of which there are thousands of instances. The 7 W B is a Texas brand, as are the 3 R and the 3 J. Of course the same tricks of uniting the strokes are likely to be employed wherever possible, as in this *Y 4 Connected*.

A single letter or numeral may be leaned to one side or another, in which case its name acquires a prefix. Thus this is not the simple T brand, but the *Tilting T* brand, or the *Toppling T*, or *Tumbling T*.

Very often, however, the letters or numerals, being as human as their creators, turn out to be downright lazy. In that event we say so. This brand is the *Lazy 2*, just as any other letter or numeral—or person—lying persistently on its back would be correctly dubbed lazy.

We have already seen how initials are made to "fly" merely by adding little wings to them. For some odd reason, however, numerals are almost never made to fly in the pyroglyphics of cattledom. But both initials and numerals apparently can become crippled, or a trifle distorted, much as a man might drag along a lame foot. Thus here is the *Drag 7* brand, made by dragging its downstroke out a bit. Any design that can thus be made to "drag" in its apparent progress is named so.

You have now read brief discussions and seen samples of the several elementary types of cattle brands, the generalized forms on which the most complicated designs are likely to be constructed—geometric lines, pictured objects, letters, numerals, symbols.

Now it is time to consider the infinitely varied *combinations* of these, for they have been put together with amazing ingenuity. Grouped, they suggest hieroglyphics of some pre-Christian era, perhaps from an ancient Egyptian tomb, or from the rock pictographs left by our own prehistoric Indians. No stranger, however erudite, can understand them at first.

The following pages present a few brands (remember, there are *millions*) which for one reason or another are better known than others, or are representative of the classifications under which they fall. Only the names of the brands (if any), not the stories back of them, are given here, but consider the probable folklore and folk-*life* behind each. Finally, in the popular custom of the day, you are invited to make a game of it: see how many of these brand names you can read or guess before referring to the answers at the end of the book. If you can name seventy-five percent of them correctly, you are well on your way toward being an expert in range pyroglyphics.

1.   2.   3.   4.   5.

6.   7.   8.   9.   10.

11.   12.   13.   14.   15.

16.   17.   18.   19.   20.

21.   22.   23.   24.   25.

26.   27.   28.   29.   30.

31.

32.

33.

34.

35.

36.

37.

38.

39.

40.

41.

42.

43.

44.

45.

46.

47.

48.

49.

50.

See page 242 for answers.

CHAPTER V

BRAND TRANSLATIONS

THE knight of old caused his silversmith, his armorer, his wood-workers, and his seamstresses to cut or sew his official coat of arms into most of the things he wore and used. The actual design was made only for looks and sentiment. Into it went a deal of imagery, much of history and symbolism that was dear to the knight's heart, even though frequently the resultant curlicues were so intricate that only he and his intimate friends understood them.

The burned escutcheons of America's saddled knights were created primarily for their practical value in identification, but inevitably they came to hold a symbolism as significant as that of European chivalry. Of the two, our cattle brands are perhaps the more honest. An armored knight leaned heavily on pomp and show, and so his coat of arms was likely to be extremely ornate, arrogantly proclaiming an importance which its owner could never achieve. But when an American rancher's coat of arms has a story back of it, you can be sure it is as real as meat and bread. Ceremony and ostentation are unknown in the legend of rangeland.

Not all the details back of the storied brands are intricate ones; indeed, most of the legends hold the charm of simplicity. They manage to touch all the chords of human emotion. They may be fantastic, or silly, or sad, or queer, or dramatic, or ironic. Many, many of them are love stories. And best of all perhaps are those which reflect the incomparable American sense of humor.

As this chapter is being written, for excellent instance, *The Arizona Republic* carries a news item about Dr. F. F. Schmidt of Douglas, Arizona, and his new herd of cattle. Dr. Schmidt is a veterinarian. For several months he has been engaged in vaccination and dipping work at railroad stock pens on the international border where thousands of Mexican cattle are shipped into the United States. In the unavoidable rush and crush there, quite a few valuable animals suffer broken legs, and normally these hapless creatures are shot, then tossed into an incinerator to be destroyed.

Dr. Schmidt, however, began buying each broken-legged animal for little or nothing. Forthwith he set the leg in a solid cast, trucked the "patient" to his own ranch, waited thirty to sixty days and lo—a healthy cow!

Registered brand for the redeemed herd is in the shape of a crutch.

It is told that a lusty young cowpuncher named Burk Burnett was addicted to poker and that he got into a game at Fort Worth, Texas, with a rancher who liked to take a chance. The game lasted well into the morning hours, with Burk taking most of the hands. Pretty soon Burk had all the rancher's money, his watch, knife, gun and hat.

"By glory, I'll bet my ranch and all its cows against your pile, on the next hand!" exclaimed the rancher desperately.

"All right," agreed Burk. "It's winner take all."

The rancher lost again, and so his name is lost now in obscurity. But Burk Burnett never even went to bed that night. He rode out at dawn and began branding all his newly acquired

cattle 6666. Four sixes was the poker hand with which he had
won the herd.

If you know the West Texas country you'll know that Burk-
burnett is a town there today. You'll know that cowboy Burk
continued to prosper. Not only did his 6666 cows multiply, but
along came another lucky plunger and struck oil on Burk's
land, so that Burk became immensely wealthy. The oil field
spread, bringing millions of dollars to the Texas Panhandle
country, and cows branded 6666 often were seen wandering
in the streets of such oil towns as Borger, notorious for its sudden wealth and for its sudden crimes. Oil derricks carried signs
that read 6666. Wagons, trucks, passenger cars, tanks, all manner of things were branded with four sixes. The erstwhile cowboy's personal stationery bore the magic brand. Texas Christian
University profited ultimately by a money endowment from
the fortune originating in the six of hearts, six of spades, six of
diamonds and six of clubs. Four Sixes became a legend of
grandeur along with such other famed Texas ranch names as
XIT, Goodnight, and King. Four Sixes and Burk Burnett
are still synonyms for importance in West Texas business
life.

As importance was achieved, however, the historic poker
game seemed to shrink in dignity. It is all right for a mere cowwaddy to play poker and be either lucky or unlucky—he can
do so and still command all the respect he needs. But when
people remember that a Big Man started toward bigness by
being a lucky gambler, the past seems best forgotten, or at least
glossed over, so that after years of prideful and chuckling ac-
ceptance the story of Burk Burnett's poker hand is now frequently denied. It has become *lèse majesté*.

No matter. The story lives, whether it's true or not, and

regardless of the fact that the cowboy himself has passed on. S. Burk Burnett recorded the 6666 brand in Wichita County, Texas, on September 22, 1885, and in Carson County in November 1908. At this writing it is still carried by about twenty-five thousand head of cattle, roaming over three hundred thousand acres. Just try to convince the old-timers that Burk didn't get his start with a poker hand. Just try!

Years ago in northern Arizona many cattle wore a brand which was read Up Y Down Y Bar. Thievery was not uncommon and brands were sometimes placed on calves which had not reached the maverick stage.

Early one morning a T V Bar rider, noticing a small fire some distance away, rode over to see if by chance some cowboy was putting the wrong sign of ownership on a calf. Approaching unnoticed in the early shadows of dawn, he witnessed a scene which impressed him greatly. No squirming calf was tied and waiting for the hot iron to be applied; in fact, there was no iron in the fire.

Kneeling beside his bed roll, a man was reverently offering his morning prayer. The rider recognized T. N. Porter, a devout Mormon cattleman, owner of the Up Y Down Y Bar.

Linking the man with his brand and the religious scene, the rider started calling Porter's brand the "Lord's Prayer", and the name stuck. Until many years later when Porter sold out, ropers at the roundup in dragging a Porter calf to the brand fire would call out "Lord's Prayer", and the symbol so translated was seared on the calf's hip.

Not all of the brands that figure prominently in the lore of the rangeland have been burned onto *herds* of cows. Sometimes, as in the case of Jess Hitson, a brand is created under dire stress and used only once, but lives longer than many another.

Cowboy Hitson was working alone on a Colorado ranch in July of 1868. He dropped his rope on a calf preparatory to branding it, dismounted, and was about to use his running iron when his hat suddenly jumped into the air.

"Good God'lmighty!" Jess doubtless exclaimed.

Some Indian had shot his arrow just a trifle high. Ignoring his punctured hat, Jess dropped behind the tied calf, unholstered his pistol and shot back.

More Indians came, and pretty soon Jess knew his earthly career was about to end. He wanted his boss and friends to know what happened, so even as he crouched there he took the red-hot running iron and branded his obituary on the animal's side:

7–4–68 INDIANS

HOT AS HELL

JH

That's the story as it was reasonably reconstructed three years later when, in New Mexico, a full-grown steer was sighted bearing that burned inscription. All that the Colorado folks knew was that Jess Hitson had just disappeared. But it was a trait of cowboy character that he took the trouble, even in the face of death, to comment on the weather.

Circumstance in 1856 contrived to force the Reverend R. O. Watkins into the cattle business in Texas, and tradition says that the parson strove mightily to create a wholly satisfactory brand. He was above the average in book learning; he had communion with the higher, more spiritual things. The people expected his brand to be a humdinger, or whatever a humdinger was called in those days. When he finally registered a plain *3* brand, the disappointed people asked him why.

"A Three is the finest symbol I could possibly choose," he informed them. "It stands for the Holy Trinity—Father, Son, and Holy Ghost."

To this day the *3* brand is a memorial to devout Parson Watkins, whether it is used in Texas or on some ranch sloping down to the North Pacific waves. But it seems likely that neither the parson nor his parishioners and friends ever heard of Hernando Cortez.

Cortez was centuries ahead of Watkins in wanting to honor the divine Trinity with his brand and in ingenuity while doing so. Hernando Cortez, as a matter of historical fact, brought the first cows and cowboys to this continent. In common with most of the Spanish pioneers (who had brought the first touches of civilization into our Southwest long before the Pilgrim Fathers sailed to Massachusetts) Cortez came with two main purposes in mind—to convert heathen souls to Christianity, and to grab a lot of heathen gold. Most of them, Cortez included, ultimately allowed the greed for gold to dominate the zeal for conversions, but Cortez at least maintained a superficial front of devotion to his higher cause. He brought in some horses and cattle and irons with which to brand them—the very first branding irons ever seen in the New World. It is still significant, in this nation of religious freedom which still combines the search for salvation with the search for gold, that Cortez' brand design was three crosses representing the Christian Trinity. The middle cross was larger. The whole design held balance, dignity, beauty in form and thought. It surely was more appropriate and picturesque than Parson Watkins' labored 3. Here it is:

✝┼✝

Pretty girls were as rare as diamonds on the rangeland in frontier days, and whenever one did drift into a ranch county all the cowboys went mildly berserk. Miss Lillybelle Plunkett came one year to West Texas with her father, who set up a ranch business. Miss Lillybelle was God's own gift to young manhood. Just to look at her once was spiritual manna, and to dance with her an exaltation beyond any cowpoke's fondest dream.

The saddled lads around the Plunkett ranch set in to pay tribute to the lady in the only way they knew how—with branding iron. Her long name had been shortened to plain Lil, so the boys roped every maverick in sight and burned L I L on its side. Each cowboy would drive his maverick up to Miss Lillybelle and show her what he had done. It was price enough to get a quarter hour of smiles and conversation from her, and from her viewpoint a fat promising dogie was worth a little sociability with the boys. Her private herd grew.

In fact it kept on growing. Rivalry among the cowboys became intensified. They began to bring her five or six calves or yearlings at a time, gifts branded L I L. In a year or two she had a valuable herd indeed—so she wrote back East to her former home and told the man she had left behind her. That man—smart fellow!—pulled up stakes and headed west, married Lillybelle, and immediately became prosperous on the cattle herd his rivals in love had created for him.

"Prettiest girl in seventeen counties" (and Texas counties

were large, then as now) was the dainty daughter of old man Tom Drake, cattle rancher. The boys from far and near came to court her, and because of her pa's name they gave cute little Miss Drake the nickname of Duck. She could stand a lot of masculine teasing; indeed she and her father and her proud brothers all reveled in her popularity. But one cowpuncher named Buck Custer wooed with more ardor than discretion, and so on a Sunday afternoon Miss Drake abruptly ordered him to high-tail it over the horizon and never show up at her home again.

Buck duly departed, and he was boiling inside. He was so mad he just had to get some sort of revenge. Down the trail a few miles he encountered a critter known as a hatrack. It was, in truth, an exceedingly bony calf, covered with ticks, unlovely in every possible way. Mr. Custer lifted his lariat rope and twirled a loop, made his catch, built his fire. Pretty soon he went on his way, his emotions having had at least partial release.

In a short time, of course, the Drake brothers saw the hatrack calf.

"That there is the scrawniest, ugliest animal in Texas!" one of them exclaimed. "And look what Buck Custer done to it!"

"Come on," the others said, spurring their horses.

Now as with many another bit of history, it is impossible to sift apart the facts and the fancies that compose the legend, but as days passed the young Messrs. Drake are known to have become madder and madder. One version of the story says they rode down Buck Custer and made a sieve of him with pistol bullets. Another says they had to be satisfied by taking it out on the hapless calf. But to us who are interested here only in branding lore the moral is the same. Mr. Custer had branded the ugly calf in huge letters: D U C K.

A love-struck farm boy is likely to carve his sweetheart's name or initials on any convenient tree. A sycamore is ideal, because its bark is smooth and white and clean. Similarly, the city boy may go into the park and carve out his sentiments, or just whittle it miserably and illegally on the apartment house banister rail. The young rancher setting up in business, however, is likely to register his girl's initials as his exclusive cattle brand.

There are literally hundreds of instances of love determining the selection of cattle brands. The young Tormeys in Arizona, mentioned elsewhere, form one instance. Another famous example is this brand:

The first normal but hasty guess is that some passionate young rancher wooed and perhaps wed a girl named Mae, and so burned her name on all his livestock thereafter. That's partly correct, but the young man loved a girl named not Mae but Emma. They married and began homesteading a ranch acreage. Emma died tragically. Sick at heart, the young man nevertheless forced himself as a widower to carry out most of the fine things that they had planned together, and while doing so he marked all his animals and other possessions with that *Me and Emma* brand.

Don Miguel Concho Ascarate de la Valenzuela y Peralta, an influential citizen of Mexico, once bought a big grazing acreage and started in the cattle business. From the Peralta initial P he proudly created this truly beautiful brand:

His ranch prospered, and soon his son Carlos was born. Doubly proud, Don Miguel changed his brand by adding his son's initial:

The next year his second son, Luis, was born, and the brand grew still more:

The third child was José, and so the Peralta brand became:

Fourth and last son was Mario, wherefore the final curves were added:

This all-in-the-family brand was hard on the *vaqueros* (cowboys) who had to memorize it; and surely was doubly hard on the cows because it had to be burned on with a single-hooked running iron, as tediously as an artist might make a free-hand sketch. It was, in short, an eminently impractical brand. But it tells more of Mexican character than most of the books about Mexico.

The Mexican takes life seriously from A to Z. It is not odd nor funny to Mexicans that Don Miguel made his brand grow; it is proper and right. Instead of angles and straight lines, the Mexican *ranchero* will almost always employ sweeping curves and circles in designing his brand. Often the design becomes so intricate that nobody can name it, but if you ask him what his brand is, the owner will squat gravely and sketch it for you with his finger in the sand. Courtesy bids you to remember, too, that his sketch is far more than a mark for identifying his cows; it amounts to his personal coat of arms. It takes labor and time to apply, but then labor and time are plentiful in his land.

By contrast, one of the simplest and yet one of the most beautiful brands ever to achieve fame in the old West was this:

$$\big)$$

A picturesque group of Mexicans rode to join a big roundup one year because their boss's cattle had begun to mingle with the Americans'. That mark showed on some of the wild steers corralled.

"Hey, what brand is that, Pablo?" an American called. "What's yore brand name?"

"¿Quién sabe?" replied Pablo, shrugging.

He pronounced it softly and correctly, *kee-ain sah-bay*, the idiomatic "nobody knows". The harum-scarum American cowboy sang out irreverently to his fellows, "It's the *kin savvy* brand," hence the marks are known as the *Quién sabe* or the *kin savvy* brand to this day, the pronunciation depending on the nationality of the speaker.

El Archivo de Fierros y Señales (Register of Brands and Marks), now to be found in worn and stained books in various California libraries or in offices of County Recorders, offers perhaps the best treasure house of the "fancy" Spanish and Mexican brands. Dating back before gold rush times, they speak loudly if silently of past glories, each elaborate brand stimulating the memory or the imagination, or both. They are truly as beautiful and romantic as the names of the owners themselves, and beside them are recorded these names, some of them still distinguished and renowned. One legal notation, for instance, accompanies a recorded brand and states in faded script: *Esperanza Sepulveda de Bandini—iron and señal recorded at*

request of her father, Diego Sepulveda, being gift to her.
Please let certificate express this.

Anywhere from Amarillo to Del Rio, Texas (or indeed beyond that indefinite area), you are likely to hear told in all seriousness the story of the ghost steer. If a cowboy gallops wild-eyed into camp and swears a steer "just disappeared" before his very eyes while he was chasing it, the old-time punchers will believe him. They know! If a series of violent deaths stalk a certain ranch, the older cowboys there will ride out in desperate effort to locate and kill—or at least drive away—the ghost steer. For this astounding animal still lives (although it would have to be fifty years of age or better if still in the flesh) and it is very likely to live on into the next century if the business of raising and branding range cattle endures. The superstitions concerning it can be accepted, of course, as your individual credulity may dictate, but the story had its origin in bald, tragic fact. Here is the authentic account as told by eye witnesses, including a son of the murdered man:

On January 28, 1890, at Leoncito in Brewster County, Texas, small ranch owners were having a roundup to brand calves that had been overlooked at the roundup the previous fall. Eugene Kelley was directing the work, and about three thousand animals had been brought into one herd. In the herd was a brindle bull yearling, unbranded and following no mother at the time. During the day, however, Mr. Kelley rode to a rancher named Henry Harrison Powe, one-armed Confederate veteran.

"Henry," Kelley called, "that brindle bull ain't marked, but it was following an HHP cow. That makes it yours."

H H P was the Powe brand, Powe's initials.

"I'll cut him out, then," Powe acknowledged.

About twenty minutes before this, a man named Fine Gilliland, employed by the cattle firm of Dubois & Wentworth but
not working with the roundup, had come near the branding
fire. Gilliland saw Powe cut out the brindle bull and put it in the
"cut" (separate herd, to be branded) in charge of Powe's son,
R. M. Powe. Gilliland promptly rode over to the cut.

"Has that brindle bull got a mother in the cut?" Gilliland
asked young Powe.

"No. But Mr. Kelley told my father it was an H H P bull,"
the boy answered.

"You'll play hell getting it unless your old man produces the
mother cow," Gilliland swore, and promptly drove the brindle
yearling back into the main herd.

Powe, Sr., saw the move, and so went again to Kelley, then
to Frank Rooney, who was an assistant boss, and conversed
with each. Both Kelley and Rooney declared the bull was
Powe's. Powe went into the main herd and was about to take
the bull again when Gilliland rode in to him. The two stopped
there a few seconds. Then Powe rode to the far side of the
herd and talked briefly with a rider named Manning Clements.
Next Powe opened Clements' saddle pocket and removed a
pistol, evidently one that he had borrowed. Then he quietly
went back into the herd and again drove out the brindle bull.

Gilliland, watching, spurred his horse. He dashed right at
Powe, tried to turn the bull back to the main herd. Powe insisted on hazing it toward the cut herd.

Gilliland produced a pistol from his own saddle pocket, but
did not use it at once. He stuck it in his belt, lifted a lasso and
tried to rope the bull, but missed. Both men were driving at the
bull frantically, accomplishing nothing, Powe having considerable trouble holding a pistol and his reins both in his one hand.

In desperation, Powe shot at the bull, to urge it on faster his way. The move succeeded and in a moment Gilliland was galloping behind them, red with anger.

Gilliland jerked his horse to a quick stop, dismounted, and squatted down on one knee. Then he raised his pistol and held it with both hands, aiming.

"Look out, Father, look out— My God!" Young Powe yelled the warning, but in the staccato of hoofs and the horn-like sounds from bawling cattle probably the older Powe never heard. CRACK! went Gilliland's pistol, at Powe's back.

Powe was not hit. But he heard, and glanced back. Then he too stopped and dismounted. He had a moment's delay wrapping the reins around his one arm, fumbling with his borrowed pistol meanwhile. CRACK! went Gilliland's pistol again. Other men came running, afoot and ahorse. Some were shouting. Powe's horse (named Raleigh) was frightened by the shots and began plunging, jerking Powe's arm and almost throwing the man down.

Gilliland had come running meanwhile. He was within five or six feet of the other man when Powe finally got straightened up, facing his adversary. They both shot, simultaneously, then shot again. Powe's gun was empty then, for it had held only three cartridges. Gilliland had not been hit, but Powe had.

Gilliland rushed in, grabbed Powe's pistol, and shot him again at such close range that the powder burned him.

"No! No!" somebody was yelling, but Gilliland did not heed.

Powe fell on his face, dead.

Gilliland turned then to face young R. M. Powe.

"For God's sake don't kill that boy!" Manning Clements pleaded.

Gilliland now held two pistols—his own and Powe's—and he looked up and warned Clements not to interfere. More men were shouting, running, calling. Helpless to stop him in the confusion, Clements and the other ranch workers present saw Fine Gilliland re-mount and dash away. When the excitement subsided, when Henry Harrison Powe was carried into a house and covered with a sheet, and all the exclaiming and explaining and cursing was at an end, Fine Gilliland was completely out of the territory. Rangers had to be notified to start a search for him.

The pointless killing so disturbed the other cowboys present, so dominated their conversation and their thoughts, that they went out next day and dropped a rope on the disputed bull, castrated it, built a fire and with a running iron burned large letters across the animal's entire side: M U R D E R. Then they turned the steer loose to roam at will.

Of course everybody knew about the tragedy, and nobody wanted the steer. One day it appeared on a ranch and another killing took place immediately. Cowboys were deeply affected. They drove the steer far away.

It turned up in the herd of another ranch, and bless Pat if a third killing didn't blot the record of that ranch's personnel! Meanwhile Rangers were pressing close on the trail of Fine Gilliland, and when they finally came up to him and shot him dead when he resisted arrest, the officers and posse saw the M U R D E R steer grazing less than a mile away!

That was enough.

The M U R D E R steer was an omen, a harbinger of death. It was invariably driven far off whenever it tried thereafter to wander sociably into any outfit's herd. Stories about it mushroomed everywhere. A phantom thing of incredible omniscience and menace. A ghost steer. For a decade it roamed impossibly over West Texas, then even into a wider range, metamorphosing right out of history into fiction and legend, and to this day it flashes occasionally in the misty dawn during a roundup, gallops tail-high through the mesquite in a rainstorm, snorts with the rangeland winds in a cyclone.

Oft told around chuck-wagons and campfires, on front porches and corral fences, in bunkhouses and at rodeos, in western hotel lobbies and even in schools, this is probably the best known and best loved of all the branding stories extant today.

The brand stories you will hear out West, however, are not all so well rounded and dramatic as these. After the M U R D E R narrative, some other cowhand in the group chinning there by the fire or leaning on the corral fence will be likely to ask, "Didja ever hear about th' Damned Hungry Dog brand, or th' Too Fat?" Before the session is over, you will have heard a choice selection of brand translations, and perhaps even seen the designs drawn with a finger in the sand.

The following pages of this chapter present a group of these representative brand designs and their factual or sentimental translations.

We have seen that while Spaniards and Mexicans made their brands from sentiments they considered beautiful and in forms which they considered beautiful, the American rancher was likely to make his from any sort of sentiment and in any sort of pattern. One instance is that of the fellow who came riding into the West to set up in the cow business and, so the tale goes, was concerned about his old hound dog which hadn't stood the trip very well. The hound looked gaunt and poor, so the man began branding his cattle with this D H D—for *Damned Hungry Dog.*

The one sign used perhaps more than all others in branding everywhere in the United States is some version of the *Dollar Mark.* It may be an S with one line through, two lines through, and sometimes three lines. It may include two S's, or even three. It was and still is considered a good luck symbol, probably because it hints at the primary need and hope felt in the brander's heart. A lot of simpler brands could be made over into dollar marks, and the single dollar mark itself was a wide open invitation to rustlers. T. E. Money was one rancher who used the dollar mark brand appropriately.

This brand was registered by newcomers from Iowa.

This one was launched by former patriotic sons of Ohio.

Five Babbitt brothers came West half a century ago from Cincinnati, Ohio, and honored not themselves but their home town in the initials of their *C O Bar* brand.

Former citizens of Essex, England, migrated to western America and soon were burning this design on their horses and cows.

A lone traveler, reputedly a wanted man, came into the West possessing nothing but two .45 calibre pistols. He sold these to start his herd, and began immediately to use this brand.

The creator and owner of the first brand here hoped first for a good percentage of return on his money invested in cattle, but when he lost money instead he changed his brand to this *Double Zero*.

Mr. Ford made his brand something of a rebus in this way, as did Mr. Crosby, his neighbor.

In Germany a person has always been considered fortunate if he owns a block of land. So when a German settled in the American West in 1850 and acquired a sizeable tract he started branding with this *Block X*. He said the square or block represented the land he owned and the X the house he proudly built on it. Together they symbolized the possessions dearest to his heart.

The *Wineglass H* brand was widely known around Frio County, Texas, after its recording in 1885. It was burned in an upright position until prohibitionists voted the county dry in 1896, then the owner turned his brand upside down and it became known as the *H Wineglass*.

An absent-minded gentleman entered the cattle business and selected this brand because it could not be stamped on upside down.

J. H. Barwise and rancher Mulkey made these brands, for obvious reasons.

This *I Bar Oh* ("I borrow") became the brand of a man who borrowed money to go into the cattle business.

From ranchers' favorite games have come innumerable *Seven Eleven, Keno, Seven Up, Hearts, Diamonds, Spades* and *Clubs* brands.

J. C. Studer, who got his start in life as a railroad blacksmith, has honored that manly profession in his brand, which is this pictured anvil. The Anvil Park Rodeo at Canadian, Texas, is still tribute to Studer's success as a rancher. But many others have used Anvil brands too.

A rancher named W. E. Daniels took cognizance of his own waistline when he registered this brand.

On the other hand, this Bony brand referred simply to the nickname—not the physique—of a rancher named Napoleon Bonaparte in western America.

When Pete Coffin long ago went into the cow business, he started a brand that is memorable to this day.

This was the brand of T. J. Walker because, said he, a man is a fool to try to make money raising cows. It was a Palo Pinto County, Texas, brand registered about 1882. Mr. Walker had to go gunning for pranksters who insisted on reburning his F to make it a B, on his bulls.

LX There is a famous ranch that uses the *LX* brand, but before it was originated there, it had been in use in another section of the country to indicate the year in which its owner started herding cows.

KT Cow folk all over her state knew that this was Mrs. Katie Barr's brand, and called it the *Katie Barr*.

☆ Chosen by the State of Texas was this Lone Star brand which is still burned in penitentiaries—not on prisoners but on state-owned cattle.

ΣX Grier Brothers registered this Greek letter brand, Sigma Chi. The men were not only blood brothers, but fraternity brothers as well.

Since away back in the time of King Solomon men have taken interest and pride in their Masonic order, and to this day the Masonic emblem—a square and compass—dominates all others of its kind in prestige, influence, and popularity. Men the world over are "branded" by their Masonic emblems, not for publicity but for what the square and compass design symbolizes.

Doubtless the cattle kings of ancient Egypt were Masons, but we have concrete proof of Masonry's importance on the American range. Many thousands of cows have roamed the hills and prairies here displaying this proud sign:

Brand number one in the records of Montana is a Square and Compass, registered in the name of Poindexter and Orr Livestock Co. of Dillon. This brand has an interesting history. Gold was luring people westward. Venturesome souls set out across the rough uncertain trails toward California. Leaving Arkansas with three hundred cows, thirty wagons, and seventy people, W. C. Orr headed for the Golden Bear State in 1853. He paused at the mining town of Yreka and found a good market for beef. Orr and P. H. Poindexter became partners and enjoyed a prosperous business trading beef for gold. Both of them being Masons, they selected the best known of all Masonic symbols for their brand. Several successful years followed. Gold was discovered at Bannack, Montana, in 1862. Predicting a good beef market, the partners drove a herd of steers from their California ranch and sold them in Bannack. Montana range conditions looked so promising that they returned to California, sold their ranch, and drove the stock to Montana. The P & O is today one of Montana's largest cattle spreads, and each year hundreds of calves are made to suffer momentarily while the sizzling branding iron burns an indelible square and compass on their ribs.

When asked if their brand has Masonic significance, Bert Orr, a son of the founder, answered, "We never regarded our brand as having Masonic significance, although all members during the outfit's history have been members of the Masonic order."

For many years, a small horse-iron hung in an old shop at Murrieta Hot Springs in California. The iron, a perfect square and compass, was at one time used by some Mason on his personal saddle animals. A tiny square and compass iron was used by Frank Maxwell in Arizona for fire-branding the noses of his goats and sheep. In 1900 the John Slaughter outfit at Post, Texas, put their square and compass brand on eleven thousand calves in one season. Brand records in most western states show that the symbol has been active for scores of years.

The Odd Fellows similarly have been paid tribute by loyal members who were ranchers, by burning the order's I O O F on horses and cows. The Knights of Pythias' K P is a common brand, so is the Woodmen's W O W. Knights of Columbus members often burn their stock with their beloved K C. It is probably a safe generalization to say that every important order in existence has been honored by members using its emblem for a brand.

CHAPTER VI

TOOLS AND TECHNIQUES

If the knight of the American rangeland could be said to wield any sort of sceptre, it would surely be an iron with a wooden handle at one end and a wrought design on the other. This sceptre of the saddle is called a stamping iron.

The chances are that in your home, school, or office there is at least one little desk device with letters on it in relief, backward and reversed, and an ink pad for use with this device. This common rubber stamp is the average person's tool for branding his letters, papers or personal effects. Use of it is precisely like the use of the cowboy's stamping iron, save that on the range fire is used instead of ink. As the iron's name implies, its design is literally stamped on the side of the cow, horse, or other object to be branded. In this case the brand is more than superficially indelible, for it is burned deep.

Arizona and Nevada, proud of their copper mines, have some stamping "irons" of copper. A few have been made of aluminum and various alloys. But perhaps ninety-five percent of all the stamping tools ever used have been made of common iron. In John Hale's collection of irons from all over the world, numbering in the hundreds, the half dozen or so irons of other materials stand out because of their oddity. The very name *iron*, although technically just one metal, encompasses them all.

The metal shank of the stamping iron ordinarily is a round rod about the thickness of a man's finger and the length of his

arm. Exact thickness and length are unimportant and vary
slightly from place to place, blacksmith to blacksmith. A few
irons with square shanks, double shanks, or twisted shanks are
seen, but these are unduly "fancy" or freakish. (Still, if you
want to dress up your stamping iron with a lot of decorative
twists and designs between handle and brand, you can be sure
nobody will object.)

The handle is likely to be a cylinder of wood two to three
inches thick and four to eight inches long, at the start. Wood
does not conduct heat readily, protects the brander's hands.
Hardwood—oak or mesquite or ironwood or hickory—is best.
No matter which is used, though, somebody is going to let the
wooden handle burn some day, or it will become dry and crack,
and split off when the horse steps on it. Against that day many
ranchers make the shank a few inches longer at the start, curl
a two or three-inch eye in it for a handle and for hanging on a
nail at home, and then hope they don't get burned while using
it. If the shank is long enough in the first place, they won't get
burned.

A piece of iron rod of correct length is worth maybe two bits
at the trading post over yonder in Skeleton Canyon, and almost
any cowpoke could twist on the handle or an eye himself. But
it takes considerable skill to work out the actual brand design
and weld it to the shank, and for this a blacksmith—amateur
or professional, preferably the latter—must be employed. Accordingly, the cost of the stamping iron jumps quickly from
two bits to an average of about ten dollars. Naturally, cost
depends on the intricacy of your design, and on how well you
know the blacksmith or how friendly he is toward you. If
your brand is a plain Drag 7, we'll say, he could hammer a seven
out on his anvil and curve its tail a little without even blowing

up his fire, and charge you maybe a dollar or two. But if your brand is a Pot Hooks and Saddle Bags design, the smithy will be heating and cutting and pounding and cursing all morning, and your bill will be a chew of tobacco plus seventeen dollars and fifty cents.

Material for the stamping part will be a strap metal—nearly always iron—of about quarter-inch thickness and one half to one inch width. The smithy may flatten out a round bar to make this for you. Many a good stamping iron has been fashioned of an old wagon tire, with laborious cutting and hammering, and probably not one iron in ten is ever made from fresh new metal. Some come from cast-off pieces about the ranch or the blacksmith's junk pile. The blacksmith's workmanship is not to be laughed at. He can't slap out a stamping iron just any old way. He knows its actual burning edges must be "square": that is, flat, or in an exact plane, as is a column or page of printer's type. Every part of every letter or design must be uniformly "type-high". This alone insures a quick, clean, readable brand that can be applied with minimum effort. Achieving this on an iron amounts to artistry as well as work.

Size of the wrought design is not standardized, save that it must be large enough for the burned brand to be read easily at several feet distance, and yet as small as possible, so as not to damage a valuable hide any more than necessary. Irons for horses and smaller animals such as sheep and goats may be as small as two inches. Most cattle brands are three to five inches across. A man's hand, fingers spread, will cover most stock brands. If the branding is done neatly, this can be read a hundred feet away or better, depending on dust, sweat, rain, snow, and eyes.

Now the actual *technique* of stamp branding would seem to need no description inasmuch as men have been branding their animals and other things for a known four thousand years. And yet—each year brings on its young men, its new generation, its fellows who through hope and circumstance have suddenly become owners of one or more animals which should be branded, and who may chance to know nothing of the actual use of the iron. In addition, there is a certain academic interest in the procedure.

The procedure is simple. First, build a fire. Modern efficiency sometimes dictates carrying a blow-torch and gasoline burners for quick heating of irons, but this is not common. Any wood fire will do, or any coal fire, or even oil fire, just so it's a fire. The "proper" and traditional way is to build a fire down on the ground from cow chips and whatever wood is available. Hot glowing coals heat the irons quicker and cleaner than flames. Set the iron right in the hottest glowing coals for a few minutes.

Caution should be exercised so that the iron is neither too hot nor too cold, and it is difficult to tell the novice just what the proper heat is. Only satisfactory thermometer in the matter is plain old judgment born of experience. The surface of the hide alone should be scorched; it will subsequently peel and leave permanent markings. Deep burning is cruel and unnecessary, likely to cause sores. We have seen incompetent branders hold an iron on and on and on, while the smoke curled and the flesh fried and the animal bawled in agony. We have also seen considerate, sensible men strike such branders with their fists; and a group of Oklahoma cowpunchers once branded a man named Ed Pool on his own rump because of his persistent cruelty to steers in branding. If Brother Pool is still living, he still has that souvenir, for the irate punchers didn't piddle with him.

There is no law dictating the exact spot on a cow's hide for the branding to be done; it is a matter of individual choice. And yet perhaps eighty or ninety percent of all range cattle are burned on the left hip, so well established is that spot. Nobody knows exactly why the left side was chosen, but perhaps the guess of Colonel Jack Potter of Clayton, New Mexico, is as good as any. Col. Potter, who made a trail drive from Texas to Montana in 1882 at the age of seventeen, and made numerous drives thereafter, says that cattle have a peculiar habit of milling more to the left than to the right, hence brands on their left sides would be more visible to cowboys inside the roundup herds.

The iron must not be allowed to slip while applying, or the brand will be blotched and useless. Face of the iron can be kept free of burnt hair and flesh by rubbing it in the ground after each application.

Not many ranchers bother to disinfect or treat a brand burn in any way, but if the animal is valuable enough to merit extra caution, linseed or other cooling oils can be applied to the burn.

A great deal of misinformation, much of it amusing, has long been extant about that secondary tool of the cattle brander—the running iron.

Writers of western fiction, whose travels westward have extended no farther than Niagara Falls, sometimes refer to a fugitive's gun as a "running iron". Because branded letters that have little legs and feet are said to run, a running iron is thought to be a special tool used for making just these brands. Still other persons with some justification believe that a running iron is the branding tool exclusively of the thief who steals cattle, re-marks them, and then runs lest he be caught and hanged.

In truth, a running iron is simply a round iron rod with a hook or quick curve on the end. Except that it has no barb, it resembles a giant fishhook. It usually is of quarter-inch, three-eighths, or half-inch metal. The straight, shank part of it is usually from two to three feet long, and it may or may not have a wooden handle affixed, like the stamping iron.

Sole purpose of the running iron is identically that of the stamping iron: to brand cattle or other stock—but in a different way. The stamping iron is the formal sceptre or seal of the saddled knight, with which in one motion he stamps his coat of arms on the animal's hide. The running iron is a fiery pencil with which he must not stamp but *draw* or sketch that coat of arms, using as many motions and strokes as necessary to make each straight line and curve of the finished design. The curved hook of the running iron, very hot, slips along the hairy hide of the cow easily, *S-s-s-s-ing* as it goes, singeing and frying and creating a hellish smell. From this motion comes the word "running". More time is required to use the running iron, but it has more latitude.

"Characters with extremely acute angles should be avoided if a stamping iron is used," says Farmers Bulletin No. 1600, U. S. Department of Agriculture, "because the heat of the iron may cause a blotch instead of showing the lines composing the brand. Open letters such as O, C, D, P, and Q can be made distinctly with a stamping iron. Such letters as A, M, N, W, and X can usually be made with a running iron by making the required number of applications of the iron to complete the letter."

The bulletin author means that it is relatively easier to make straight lines with a running iron than curved lines, and this surely is true. It does not follow, moreover, that the angled letters have no part in stamped designs; the majority of stamping irons do contain angles, and a careful and experienced cowboy need not blotch the brand in applying it. Indeed, if he does so blotch it, he is pretty sure to get bawled out by his fellows, then by his boss, and he deserves what he gets. A running iron will slip easily and blotch a brand, and it is almost impossible to run two brands uniform in size and artistry. Disfiguring and cruel brands can be made easily with a running iron, and heartless cowboys occasionally lasso a yearling and "draw" ridiculous designs all over it, in order to insult some enemy rancher, or just out of plain cussedness. Some men have developed truly remarkable skill with a running iron, and one old-timer has declared, significantly, "I can take an iron rod, bend one end into a half circle and burn a damn sight better brand than I can draw on paper with a pencil."

The running iron is used mainly because it is convenient and cheap. A stamping iron is a heavy tool. On a saddle it will bounce and flop around annoyingly, gouge the horse's flank, hook on shrubbery and vines, generally be a nuisance unless sheathed and tied on with great care, and even then it is in the way. The shorter, lighter running iron is much less in the way and it can be made by any cowboy or cowgirl who can steal the rod from the end gate of a wagon.

The running iron is reduced perhaps to the simplest possible terms by the cowboy who tosses a saddle cinch-ring into the fire, watches it turn red, then makes a grip handle for it of a small green limb bent double. If he's skilled he can brand a cow with that, and many a steer has known no other. This, however, is not easy, is an emergency measure at best. The regular running iron tied to the saddle strings or stuck in a saddle pocket is far better, if the standard stamping iron cannot be had.

But the running iron is also an ideal pencil for that rewrite man known as the rustler and so is frowned upon in many sections, notably in Texas where the mere possession of one is illegal.

Now it may be that some future edition of this book will have to be revised considerably to accord prominent place to a newfangled business known as toothbrush branding.

Undeniably some ranchers today are branding their animals not with hot irons but with "hot" chemicals. In one revolutionary gesture these men are throwing aside the tools of four thousand years, discarding the romantic sceptre of range heraldry, introducing modern "efficient" chemicals applied as simply and painlessly as you would paint a house number over your front steps. The newspaper feature-writers went mildly berserk at the news a few years back. "Branding irons obsolete!" one syndicated writer proclaimed. "All over the West hot iron branding is now in the discard, and painless, easier chemical branding is the new method."

The energetic writer went off half-cocked. Quite a few *experiments* were being made with chemical branding and some of those experiments showed promise of success. Namely, they proved that you could truly brand a cow with chemicals instead of fire if you wanted to. But the writer failed to take human nature into consideration, and neglected to wait a few years and see the effects of chemical brands. The new process is not as revolutionary—yet—as it promised to be. A great majority of ranchers, including most of those who stooped to try it, have given it up with a certain contempt.

It may be that sheer force of social pressure, tradition and habit and all that, accounted for the fact that ranchers accepted chemical branding very gingerly and then threw it aside, for the scientific reports on the matter persist in saying that it is practical and good. The austere United States Department of Agriculture, which exists only to help farmers and ranchers, in its bulletin on the matter states cagily that "the cold brand is more conveniently applied, especially when only a few animals are to be branded, and the process is presumably less painful." Then the bulletin goes on for pages and pages describing hot iron branding.

The "paint" is applied with either a brush or a stamping iron, the latter much like the conventional stamping iron already described. Only difference is that the handle of course may be shorter, since insulation from heat is not necessary. The wrought design of the cold stamping iron is dipped into branding liquid about one-eighth inch deep, then pressed on the cow's hide in exactly the same manner as in heat branding. This liquid is quick to destroy the surface hair and flesh and in most cases does leave a satisfactory scar. Some users claim that bronze is a better metal for cold stamping than iron; others deny this.

The chemical solution used is frequently built upon a base of common croton oil, known for years as a powerful purgative. This blistering extract is derived from seeds of the croton plant, a large genus of trees and shrubs. Acids are generally held unsatisfactory because their action is so prolonged as to destroy too much tissue and so blotch the brand.

Several mixtures are in use. Dr. A. J. Stockenburg of Lindsborg, Kansas, created one the main ingredient of which was sodium hydroxide, a caustic, on a coal tar base. It seemed to have some merits above the croton oil mixtures, although croton oil and sodium hydroxide are sometimes used together. Dr.

Stockenburg's formula was purchased by a nationally known manufacturer of stock remedies, and a patented product offered on the market. The manufacturer made the cautious statement that the product was "not a fool-proof method of branding at all, but with proper handling is easier, quicker, and more humane than use of the hot iron. When properly applied the fluid appears to cause a mild burning or itching sensation for about fifteen or twenty minutes, after which there is no apparent feeling in the brand. A scab is formed in a few days, scabbing off in about thirty days."

The principal difficulty (beyond that of overcoming tradition) seemed to be that the fluid had to be kept at a temperature of about eighty degrees Fahrenheit for proper handling. If allowed to drop to a lower temperature, too much would adhere to the brush or iron, causing blotched brands. Thus a fire would be necessary in a great many cases to warm a can of the fluid, and care would be necessary then in order not to get it too hot. The fluid might all be used up in the middle of a roundup when nobody had time to ride in to town or write back to Kansas City or somewhere for another can. The chemical might deteriorate from lack of use, or be spilled, or be mistaken by already drunk cowboys for some new and possibly exhilarating "likker". In short, it is not at all difficult—for one who knows cow folk—to envision ranchers trying the new-fangled chemical, then growling "To hell with it!" and reaching for the age-old hot branding iron.

Number One tool of the cowboy, before even the branding iron, is the common pocket knife. Indeed, it is an indispensable item in every normal American boy's or man's pocket, and without it he is eternally handicapped or makes a nuisance of himself by borrowing someone else's. The knife may be almost any conceivable sort from the dainty pearl-handled pencil sharpener to the lethal weapon made famous by James Bowie. In actual practice on the cattle range it is likely to be a two-, three-, or four-bladed thing of excellent steel, about four inches long and with carved horn sides. The main blade will come to a sharp point and have an edge almost good enough to shave with. Good steel nowadays is truly good and a knife that will last a man five to ten years is not uncommon and need cost no more than a dollar or two.[1] It will be ideal for, say, picking the owner's teeth, cutting his barbecued beef, boring a new hole in his saddle girth strap, and scraping ticks from a calf, and it may be used for all of those services several times in one day without the formality of washing.

So far as this discussion is concerned, however, the cowboy's knife is a thing with which to castrate bulls and to mark ears As such, it may be any reasonable kind of knife just so it is convenient and sharp, although a thin-bladed variety is always best. Special knives for castrating and ear-marking can be purchased, but they are unnecessary. Absolute sharpness (any dull knife is an abomination anywhere) and reasonable cleanliness are about all the rancher asks.

Castration and its allied operation, spaying, are two of the processes of ranch life which the motion pictures and fiction writers have studiously ignored; this is just as well, for the processes can not be called romantic and they hold little interest

---

[1] John Barry of Minden, Texas, uncle of co-author Arnold here, carried a certain keen-bladed pocket knife as early as 1910. When Arnold visited him in 1939 Uncle Johnny was whittling with that same knife. It had seen farm and ranch service over all that time, was still dependable.

for the person merely seeking a western thrill. On the other hand, a great many city folk are surprisingly ignorant about the matter. Adult men and women, even college graduates, often think that the knife is somehow used with the hot iron only for branding. They are amazed to learn that cowboys grouped around a thrown bull are doing anything besides marking it for identification. In these good people's lives, "castrate" both as a process and a word has been largely taboo. But it is highly important on the range, is closely associated with our main theme, which is branding.

The meat of a steer is more refined, more tender and tasty and altogether better developed, and hence more valuable, than is the meat of a bull. A bull two years of age or older will usually have heavier crests and heavier forequarters than hindquarters, and as such is classed as a "bologna bull" because his meat quality is low. Unspayed or "open" heifers are slow to fatten properly, have less desirable meat than heifers that are spayed. Fat two-year-old spayed heifers produce meat virtually as good as meat from steers of the same age. Spaying also serves to cull out heifers held undesirable for breeding. Spaying further simplifies the herd work in that it makes separation of the undesirable breeding heifers from the bulls unnecessary. Buyers necessarily are suspicious of unspayed heifers offered on the market, fearing that the heifers may be with calf and hence of little value, and so lower their prices accordingly.

As with branding, there are two main ways of handling the stock for castrating and spaying: the animal may be roped, thrown and held firmly during the operation, or it may be placed in a "squeeze" chute. By far the greater number of animals, however, are castrated or spayed by "main strength and awkwardness"; the ranch hands simply catch a bull and render him helpless with their own hands, kneel on him and go to work.

Because hemorrhage or bleeding is more profuse as the bull gets older, castration is best done when the animal is under eight months of age, although it may be and frequently is done to full grown bulls. Reasonable cleanliness should be insisted upon lest infection strike the castrated animal and kill it. If the work is done in fly season it is essential to apply some sort of fly repellent. Common in the warmer sections of the country is that also highly unromantic infestation known as screwworms or maggots, these being the larvae of certain flies.

In valuable dairy herds and on small ranches, a method of "bloodless castration" is being employed more and more, and has definite advantages. The method requires special pincers or clamps which may be purchased at little cost from any reliable dealer handling stockmen's supplies, and simple instructions come with them.

Spaying of heifers is not as simple as castrating bulls. Comparatively few ranch men spay their heifers themselves, and the services of veterinarians—or at least of experienced cattle spayers—are here recommended.

Another operation closely allied with branding, castrating and spaying is that of de-horning. Nature in her wisdom endowed most cattle with horns, for use as weapons of protection against such predators as panthers and wolves, but in the commercial raising of cattle in ranch herds horns are not only unnecessary but a distinct disadvantage. The justly renowned Texas Longhorn steer—whose headpiece sometimes extended right and left like bicycle handle bars for as much as eight feet

—is now just a museum piece.[1] Finer, high-bred or "highbrow" cows—in the slang of the day—have been developed, animals with more and better meat on them than the Longhorn ever had, but in spite of this modern skill at breeding the aristocratic beeves are likely to have dangerous horns and muscles for using them. The horns not only endanger men and horses who work with cattle, they harm the cattle themselves. Bulls or steers or heifers with horns start fighting, or go on stampede, and do as instinct directs them. They try to gore every enemy in sight. Shipping of horned cattle invariably results in bruised carcasses, and bruises on meat greatly lower its money value at the market. Cowhides may be damaged by horns also. In general, de-horned cattle bring from twenty-five cents to seventy-five cents more a hundredweight on the market than do horned cattle of similar quality and condition, so that if a rancher can figure in the time and manpower to do de-horning, he is that much ahead.

De-horning can be achieved in any one of three ways:

1. By prevention. Growth of horns can be prevented by properly applying caustic soda or potash to young calves' heads, and this method is satisfactory for small herds that can be kept under close observation. Very young calves with only "buttons" for horns are best subjects for this. Hold the calf firmly. Clip the hair from around the base of the "button" horn, apply petrolatum to prevent the caustic from burning the skin, moisten one end of the caustic and apply it to the "button". Two or three applications are necessary, with the

[1] Literally that. A few years ago the federal government had a hard time finding even half a dozen pure Longhorns, hardy creatures once raised in the Southwest by the hundreds of thousands. But a few of pure strain were found in old Mexico and brought to this country for breeding, so that the historic species might not be entirely lost.

caustic allowed to dry between applications. Hold the caustic not with the bare hand but with a sheath of cotton or paper to prevent injury to your own flesh.

A hard metal spoon or chisel is sometimes used as a gouge to remove calves' "buttons" and prevent growth, but the caustic method is generally preferred.

2. By sawing. In this operation, the horn is simply sawed off at a point about one-quarter inch below the junction of the horn with the hide. Cutting here will enable the hide to grow over the horn stub and prevent re-growth of the horn cells. Any good short hand-saw can be used for this, but best are the inexpensive saws made especially for this purpose.

3. By clipping. Mechanical de-horners of several kinds can be purchased from stockmen's supply stores. These are simply knives that clip off the horn quickly by powerful leverage from handles. There is a special device, too, for de-horning calves mechanically. In clipping, as in sawing, the horn should be cut below the hide line, to prevent re-growth.

In any event, whether de-horning is done by caustic or mechanical means, infection is likely to result if the wounds are not kept clean or if flies are present and not repelled. De-horning, like castration, should be done only in cool or cold weather, and treatment for prevention and cure of infection is exactly the same as for that following castration. Special care should be given calves de-horned with caustic. Such calves should be kept out of rain for a few days after the operation.

For use on a few animals, especially valuable breed bulls and heifers where conventional branding and ear cutting would mar the outward "show" perfection, three other methods of marking for identification have come into limited use. One is the simple locking on of a neck chain, and this may be seen on a prize bull or two at any county fair. Second method is ear-tagging, in which metal tags or buttons are clamped into the animals' ears, each tag carrying its name or number. Third method is ear-tattooing, whereby any design is inked indelibly under the inner skin of the ear, just as flags and bleeding hearts and daggers and naked girls are tattooed on the chests of lusty, sentimental sailors. The tattooing process is essentially the same for bull or seaman; special needles and inks must be used.

Neck chains, ear-tags, and tattooing instruments can be purchased from stockmen's supply stores.

On occasions, highly bred show animals are branded by burning half-inch numerals not on the hide but on the horns. This avoids disfigurement, is a convenience for identifying in stock shows and auction rings, but on the whole is of little practical value as branding goes.

Far above all other secondary means of marking animals, however, is the practice of marking them by cutting the ears. Ear-marking of cattle is almost as universal as branding. The marking is done simply by cutting a specific notch or slit in one or both the animal's ears, using a sharp knife. A common practice is for ranchers to castrate, vaccinate, de-horn, brand and ear-mark an animal all at one throwing or at one "squeezing" (in the chute to be described below). A ranch's ear-mark is registered along with the brand and is similarly protected by law, although there are not nearly so many different kinds of ear-marks as of brands, naturally.

Ear-marks are held an advantageous supplement to brands because a man can see the mark while directly in front of or behind the marked animal, and so identify it. It is necessary to get a side view in order to see the brand. Sometimes in the dust kicked up by a herd ear-marks are visible when a brand isn't. Long hair on the animal in winter may overlap the brand and make it hard to read, in which case the ear-mark becomes valuable as a supplement. Many a weary cowpuncher would have to ride an aggregate of five or fifteen extra miles a day just getting close to stock and turning them so he could read their brands, if the stock lacked ear-marks.

These chiseled ears are an especial godsend to the tired rider in rough brushy country, checking stock from the opposite side of a deep canyon; he can't quite make out the brand, but probably he can identify the ear-mark. He may be only a few yards from the cows in direct air line, but to get any closer he'd have to be a bird or have to ride, scramble and roll down a quarter-mile slope and work back up another quarter-mile steep enough to require a ladder, or he'd have to go one, two or five miles around. Some cowmen save many miles of hard riding by carrying a telescope in their saddle bags; through this simple, inexpensive instrument both brands and ear-marks can be read at great distance, and because of brush, or overlapping hair on the rumps, the ear again can be read farther than the brands. In spite of all these advantages, however, a great many ranchers never bother to do any ear-marking at all.

The cartilage of a cow's ear is tough, and this time the knife *must* be very sharp if a clean cut is to be made. Many ingenious marks have been devised by cattlemen. Crop, overslope, underslope, split, bit, swallow fork, steeple fork, oversharp, undersharp, are some of the descriptive terms given common ear-marks. These are by no means as picturesque as brands and they have no whit of sentiment attached to them, which may be why many ranchers ignore ear-marks entirely and why so little is heard of them in the story books. Another reason is that men have pride in their animals, and disfigured ears mar their clean, neat appearance.

Below are the nine common ear-marks named above; see if you can identify them before reading their names in the next paragraph:

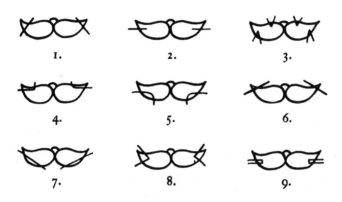

1.   2.   3.

4.   5.   6.

7.   8.   9.

Number 1 is a *crop*; 2 is a *split*; 3 is a *bit*, under or over (either or both may be used on the same ear); 4 is the *overslope*; 5 is the *underslope*; 6 is the *oversharp*; 7 is the *undersharp*; 8 is the *swallow fork*; 9 is the *steeple fork*. It is obvious that when ears are flopping, sagging, hanging, and perhaps unkempt with dirt and hair, these marks also would be difficult to identify without very close inspection. (Ear-marks and their names, as used here, are from a bulletin of the United States Department of Agriculture. Names may vary from section to section.)

A great many people have the impression that cattle are the only animals ever to be branded. Some marking process, however, has been used on many other animals, including horses, sheep, goats, mules, camels, llamas, alpacas, elephants, buffalo, bison, hogs, dogs, cats, ducks, chickens, turkeys, geese, swans, even grasshoppers and bees. Not all of them, of course, could be branded with fire.

Second in branding interest to the rancher is the marking of his horses. Very seldom does a man feel as impersonal or unsympathetic toward a horse as he does toward a cow. He may be able to burn a steer, hear the animal bawl with fear and pain, and see the ugly mark throughout its life, and still feel no compunction whatsoever. But a man does not want his horses marred in the slightest. He brands them only when absolutely necessary. Usually a horse brand is half the size of a cattle brand, or even smaller. Often it is different from the cattle brand, even on the same ranch.

A cow's hip is one of the ugliest things in animate nature, but a horse's hip is one of the prettiest and most graceful. This probably accounts for the custom of branding horses on the shoulder, where the mark can still be seen but will least offend the human eye. Not all owners brand their horses on the shoulder, but the genuine horse lovers do.

The tools and techniques of branding horses are identical with those of branding cows, save that stamping irons are smaller, and extra caution is exercised so as not to harm the more valuable horse. Because a horse is used under saddle or harness, cuts, abrasions, scars and sores created by careless lassoing and throwing are to be avoided. Accordingly, more men usually are required to brand a horse, and much more care. Nervous shock is a consideration, too, in horse branding. A stolid old steer or heifer has no future save to go off and graze and rest, but a horse must be put back in service tomorrow, and is more "high-strung" anyway. Gentleness in branding horses

will always pay. Where practical, a squeeze chute, which holds
the horse erect but unable to plunge and buck, will be a good
investment. Otherwise the force of men and ropes must be
employed. A horse has silkier, lighter hair than a cow, and
tenderer skin; the iron must not be too hot, nor applied too
long.

Best horse branding epic in American history probably is
that which took place near San Angelo, Texas, during the Boer
War. March and Thornton, a horse and mule firm, contracted
to furnish the English government twenty-five thousand horses.
The animals were rounded up from all parts of the Rio Grande
range country, mustangs that were indeed woolly and wild.
The English did not want their animals mutilated, but under
Texas law no horse could be shipped without a brand. As a
result, March and Thornton's cowboys had the task of lassoing,
holding and fire-marking all of those twenty-five thousand
tough mustangs.

The brand selected was a small U, burned on a hip. Nobody
now remembers that the U had any special significance. Perhaps it was chosen because it was easily made, had no angles or
points that might burn too deeply and leave ugly scars. Since
then, however, the U brand has been used on countless other
horses.

Those "war horses" brought approximately twenty-five dollars a head and were shipped by train to Charleston, South
Carolina, where they were loaded on boats for Sydney in far
away Australia. Eight of the Texas cowboys were hired to
accompany the boatloads of horses around the world, and at
Sydney begin breaking the animals for cavalry use. These
bronco busters made such a success of this enterprise that the
English government wined and dined them royally, paid them

well and enabled some of them to get a good start in life. Three of them are successful cattlemen in Australia today.[1]

Sheep, being too woolly to brand indelibly (like horses or cows), without great trouble, usually are branded through the thin wool of the nose, necessarily with very small brands. Temporary brands or marks are just painted on the sheep, on top of their wool; this serves as an aid in separating the breed rams from the others, in checking the wool production and increase of specific herds, and otherwise in handling the sheep. In general, the same considerations apply to handling goats as well.

It would serve no practical purpose here to give detailed instructions for branding other domestic animals, or wild ones. Simple instructions are available from any competent veterinary or experienced stockman, or usually from stores selling stockmen's supplies. Government pamphlets offer helps, too.

The reader will be interested, however, in both the process and the reasons for branding grasshoppers and bees. In point of fact, these experiences appear to be new. A. M. Hengy, apiarist residing at Oroville, California, developed valuable queen bees which he wanted to claim as exclusively his and sell as his exclusive "stock". He evolved a simple way of branding them with a pigment so as to do them no harm.

Grasshoppers presented a more important problem. Branding of them was actively encouraged by cattle raisers themselves. In fact it is said that a cattle rancher suggested the idea to a distracted federal government scientist who was leading the warfare on the flying pests.

Grasshoppers settled down on a wide rangeland and ate up

[1] For details of this episode the authors are grateful to William Tip Arnold of Henderson, Texas, who as a young man then took part in the horse roundup and branding spree.

every inch of grass. Naturally the cattle all had to be moved. Immediately, however, the hoppers flew over to a farm district and devoured everything there almost over night. The word "everything" is used advisedly; unless you have experienced a grasshopper invasion you cannot imagine the devastation they cause. In this instance peach and apricot trees were quickly stripped of their foliage and the developing fruit consumed. Only the seeds of the fruit were left dangling on naked twigs. Grapevines were left bare, ornamental shrubs and hedges were reduced to dark brown skeletons. Householders were able to enter or leave their homes only over thousands of the invaders. Crawling over railroads, the hoppers were squashed by engines, so that the rails became slippery, slowing and even halting the progress of transcontinental trains. So many of the pests were mashed on pavements that they caused automobiles to skid and stop.

Thus the hopper invasion became an emergency measure, not only for immediate combat but for future defense. It was in order to study the hoppers' movements, in the hope of learning how to combat them, that one hundred thousand of them were caught alive and branded. Naturally the branding was delicate and tedious because they were so small. Each was dyed with an indelible red pigment, then released. After two weeks, government agents in other counties and states were to begin making reports on the branded hoppers' spread. In this manner scientists hoped to throw valuable light on the habits of the pests.

Repeated reference has been made to branding chutes or "squeezes", used often to avoid lassoing, throwing, and holding of animals while operating on them. These chutes undeniably have some advantages, but some distinct disadvantages too. Most ranchers feel that the latter offset the former, although many chutes are employed for supplementary if not exclusive use in the operations of branding, castrating, de-horning or otherwise doctoring.

It is held only little more trouble to throw and tie an animal than to haze it into the chute in the first place. A chute is not readily portable; it cannot be carried to the animal; the animal must be driven to it. The chute costs additional money. On the other hand a chute does quickly render the animal helpless, so that any operation can be performed with minimum danger and struggling. In the long run, decision to use a chute or not is an individual problem.

A serviceable chute can be built with ordinary common-sense and whatever timbers and tools are likely to be at hand on the average ranch. If branding is to be done in the chute, one of its sides should be movable so that the animal can be held snugly but without injury, and so that animals of various sizes can be accommodated. A de-horning gate can be built at one end, so designed as to hold the head of the animal firmly.

CHAPTER VII

COWBOY CRUELTY

Most memorable thing about the first branding work a dude or a dudette witnesses is likely to be the heart-rending "BAWR-R-R-R-R!" of the calf or other animal under the hot iron. In the tenderfoot springs a horror, then a feeling of abject pity followed often by anger. This reaction is only natural. Fire is universally feared, and justly so; ingenious man in all the centuries has devised no more fiendish way to torture his fellow men than to burn them. No racks nor screws nor spreads of the Inquisition could provide sadistic pleasure equal to that of the American Indians who tied white captives naked to posts and dropped glowing coals on their bellies.

A second and almost as fiendish method of human torture, still employed in such "advanced" groups as the Japanese armies in dealing with their Chinese captives, is to mutilate a man by removing his procreative glands. This is held to be the supreme insult as well as a highly entertaining means of inflicting pain; a man's *pride* as well as his physical person can be tortured in that way, and decent folk have looked with especial horror on any form of castration since history began. Therefore, the dude or dudette, after hearing the yearling bull bawl at hot iron branding, is likely to learn that the bull is being castrated too, and then rush away in an extreme condition of nausea and indignation.

In some instances the Society for the Prevention of Cruelty

to Animals has been appealed to, without results. Undoubtedly the Society has invoked laws and social pressures to alleviate conditions for other animals suffering far less than do the range cows. But so far as the range is concerned, there is absolutely nothing the Society or anybody else can do. Unless, perhaps, it is to reason about the matter.

Imagine an inch-long burn, skin-deep, on your finger or leg.

It would of course be painful. A sudden stinging burn, an "ouch!" feeling, a hasty concern. If you are a child it would be a matter for tears and for treatment from the family kitchen —strong cold tea being about the best known remedy for fire burns—and in an hour or two the burn would be forgotten. It would remind you of its presence every time you touched it for perhaps a week. In that time it would peel, leaving maybe a permanent scar. But in general you would not be discommoded or badly hurt at all. If the burn were deliberately applied to you, your feelings—that is, your emotions—would be hurt worse than your finger or leg.

There is reason to believe that a cow does not have very well developed emotions, and so does not become indignant or angry at the branders. And, if you consider the comparative sizes of you and the bull, you will realize that a brand on a bull's side is about equal to an inch burn on your human skin. Therefore the burned animal's suffering is negligible, although in initial fear of the unknown or of the cowboys' necessary roughness in handling it, it will go "BAWR-R-R-R", its eyes will bulge alarmingly, its mouth will slaver, and its nose will snort.

We can also conclude that an animal experiences no pain as acutely as man does, even in proportion to size, for it is very likely that the animal's nervous system is not nearly so highly developed as is man's. This, at least, is the answer most sincere cattle ranchers will give you.

"The sting from the actual burn sometimes causes a calf or steer to try to lick his brand for a half hour or so after we release him," one Wyoming rancher said. "But in a little while the animal always goes calmly on about its affairs, eating grass or chewing or dozing. The shock of castration and de-horning is greater, no doubt, but even then the animals do not show any signs of extreme suffering. Most of it is fright."

It must be remembered that the same cross-section of American society, so far as morals and kindness are concerned, is to be found among ranch folk as among city residents. No typical rancher would deliberately hurt any living thing save in the absolutely necessary processes of extracting a living from nature. We cannot live without pain; pain and blood and torture and death. The very dude and dudette who turned green and indignant at the branding scene will be the first to fork a filet mignon at dinner time, and even they must know that tender steaks come from *steers* that have been deliberately killed! A favorite—if barbarous—way to kill a beef steer is to knock it in the head with an axe. Often it will bawl and snort and bleed at the nose and stagger around miserably in the process of dying. But the filet, broiled to a juicy, bloody saltiness and served with sterling silver, Haviland china and imported crystal ware, plus swing music, is delicious indeed.

Hold all of these concepts in mind before you condemn the cowboy for cruelty, and remember that the fire brand is the only successful means of identifying stock which has yet been devised.

CHAPTER VIII

THE REWRITE MAN

1.

Mr. Isaac Hobart was departing rather hurriedly from the State of Tennessee. He had been a troublesome draftee in the recent War Between the States, had finally deserted Lee's army, and after Appomattox had turned up in Nashville with no visible means of support. His means became visible, however, when he was seen to kill a man in order to rob him, wherefore Mr. Hobart was now hurrying westward.

He succeeded in leaving both his conscience and the sheriff behind him, killed one horse by running it to death, stole three others, and so continued on into East Texas. By chance he met a man there who knew that he had raped a Yankee girl after a raid in the War, so to save his neck again he had to keep on fleeing. He trekked on foot part of the time, got a job driving a mule team toward San Antonio, deserted the wagon and stole two horses and went on out beyond the Pecos River. Nobody out there had ever heard of him and no sort of sheriff or other legal restraint was to be found there. Mr. Hobart now said his name was Ike Smith, and that his business was nobody else's.

That last announcement stood, out west of the Pecos. Nobody gave a hoot what his business was so long as he attended to it exclusively. He wore rough clothes and a couple of pistols, and after a while he seemed to own a few cows. Word got around that his brand was the Three Leaf Clover, thus:

It was as good a brand as any. The region was not too populous, and if another man wanted to come in and enter the cattle business, there was room.

This Ike Smith was fierce looking. His eyes were eternally bloodshot and had a mean way of squinting when he stared appraisingly at a man—or a woman. He came into the saloon at Vinegaroon, later Langtry, Texas, owned by the notorious Justice Roy Bean, and drank more liquor than any man ought to, and sometimes Judge Bean had to beat him over the head with a bung starter or a stick of stovewood and send him on his way. But in general people let Ike Smith alone and he let them alone. He acquired the nickname of Alkali Ike and deserved it, for he lived over beyond the alkali flats and was eternally clouded with the salty pale dust from the landscape there. Other ranchers often wondered how his cattle found enough water and grass; the land he had squatted on wasn't very good. Nevertheless, his herd seemed to grow; his Three Leaf Clover brand was seen more and more.

Fifteen miles away from Ike Smith's ranch shanty lived Old Man Dubose who ran the Yes Jenny brand on his stock. Old man Dubose's wife was something of a shrew and even her husband recognized his subjugation to her, so that he said his YJ brand stood for Yes Jenny. He made the brand connected like this: **Y**
His cowboys could make it easily with stamping or running iron. His ranch became a prosperous one until Alkali Ike Smith showed up in the region, after which the YJ herd didn't seem to grow as fast as it once did.

Mr. Dubose was appalled at the few calves he found to brand during one spring roundup. It seemed to him that his increase was far below what he might have expected. So without whooping or hollering about it, he just inquired around. And yes sir, by coincidence Alkali Ike Smith's Three Leaf Clover ranch had sent a rather large herd of young animals to market.

One day the following week Mr. Dubose and two of his punchers quietly rode around the mesa, up Deadman's Canyon, over alkali flats and down into the little meadow where grazed some of Ike Smith's cows. They saw a fat yearling branded with the Clover Leaf, lassoed it and knocked it in the head. In ten minutes they had the skin pulled back off its rump.

"By God!" growled Old Man Dubose. "Just what I expected!"

"Yais sir," his two cowboys nodded, gravely.

Without another word they broiled some of the tender meat, refreshed themselves, and rode on to Ike Smith's shack several miles away.

Smith was a suspicious man. He was on his porch when Mr. Dubose and one cowboy approached, and he was holding a rifle.

"What do you want?" Ike asked his neighbors, inhospitably.

"Ike," Mr. Dubose began slowly, bluffing to kill time, "hev you seen anything of some YJ horses running loose over here? We been scouring the country for some valuable breed mares of mine."

"Ain't seen a thing," said Ike.

"Um. Waal, it's a right long spell of dry weather we're havin', ain't it?"

"Some say 'tis." Ike was still cautious. "You want anything else?"

"Just aiming to rest a minute and be neighborly, Ike. Ain't never been here before, and . . ." Mr. Dubose made quite a talk, harmless, meaningless, while both he and his cowboy companion slumped lazily in their saddles. Several minutes passed, and finally Mr. Dubose lifted his arms to stretch and yawn.

That was a signal. Instantly from around the corner of Ike Smith's house, and from Ike's rear, a lariat loop snaked out and settled around Ike's body.

The rope jerked tight just as Ike would have lifted his rifle. He never had a chance. While Mr. Dubose and his cowboy companion sat on their horses chinning, the third YJ rider had been given time to slip up to the house from the rear. Now he had rendered Mr. Hobart, alias Ike Smith, helpless.

Ike understood that the jig was up. He had slipped away from the sheriff in Tennessee. He had run fast to leave the irate East Texas behind. But here he was in the binding loop of a YJ rope, with the YJ boss now glaring at him.

The YJ men didn't make much of a ceremony of it.

"Smith," Old Man Dubose growled in requiem, "you was right smart. You took a running iron and rewrote my YJ brand into your Three Leaf Clover. You musta done it to a thousand of my cows, curlicuing my brand marks around to make yourn. You're a cussed rustler and your end has come."

Ike glared and cursed and finally whined for pity, but in a scant quarter hour the three YJ men rode away, leaving Ike dangling by the neck from a rafter inside his own miserable home. Nobody knows just how long he had to hang there before the coyotes and wolves and the carrion takers sniffed the scent of him and went in to eat whatever they wanted, but it was more than a year later when some YJ cowboys rode over again out of curiosity, and burned the cabin and its contents to the ground.

Here is how Alkali Ike rewrote the YJ brand:

One of the most famous ranchers in Mexican border history was Pete Kitchen, of about the same period as Alkali Ike and Old Man Dubose. Kitchen's stomping ground was southern Arizona. When the United States withdrew all its soldiers from the frontier to fight back East in the Civil War, most of the Arizona ranch folk ran to the towns for protection, but Pete Kitchen elected to stay on his land and fight it out with the Apache Indians who were bound to start new raids.

By sheer force of character and by making his ranch a fortress Pete carried out his plan. He had to be strong. He had to make every Mexican servant and cowboy a constantly armed soldier. One twilight as Pete sat resting on his front porch his keen eye saw an Indian bob up on a knoll six hundred feet away. Instantly Pete snatched up the rifle that stood beside him, and shot. Just one shot. But before bedtime Pete had walked out there and buried the Indian that the shot killed. Pete was that kind of man.

Now, in the course of events a certain Mexican took to rustling Pete Kitchen's stock, re-branding some and driving some off to Mexico, at great personal risk but at considerable profit even so. Pete stood it for a while, and then one day the thief took one of Pete's favorite horses. Furious, the ranch owner got in a buggy and drove after the man.

When he came back alone a few days later people knew he had caught the rustler even though he offered no explanation. Pete Kitchen would have hunted forever rather than return without his quarry. Finally somebody asked him if he did catch the thief.

"Certainly," he replied.

"Well, where is he at, then? What happened?"

"Why, he suffered a mishap. I caught him down by the Line

and started back with him, leading the stolen horse on which he was tied. Night come and I had to rest. I says to myself then, 'How can I rest and not let this rustler escape?' So I tied the man's hands behind him, tied a rope around his neck and put him astride the horse. Other end of the neck rope I tied to the limb of a tree, just keeping the slack out of it. It wasn't hurting him none, so I laid down on a blanket near by and went to sleep."

"What happened then, Mr. Kitchen?"

"Why, come daylight, doggone if I hadn't forgot to hitch the horse, and it had wandered off grazing in the night! I had a right hard time catching it again."

Up and down California all the way from Los Angeles to San Francisco are some eroded mountains that have ceased through the long centuries to be real mountains but instead are just smoothed off mounds or bulges a few hundred feet high. In early summer the rich grass on them is likely to go to seed and turn tan, so that they become overstuffed plush pieces, occasional grazing cows being the ornamental buttons on them. Back of these hills, often, are real mountains enriched with streams and redwood and oak and manzanita and all manner of lesser growths that bloom incomparably as only the shrubs and flowers of California can, and crouched in the canyons and valleys of such a beautiful region have been ranch homes for three-hundred-odd years. Long before the Yankees discovered gold at Sutter's Mill, and much longer before the movie producers discovered gold in Hollywood, Spanish dons had wrought prosperity out of these velvet hills.

Don Madariago Hipólito José del Castellana y Villaverde y Castro once owned several thousand head of cattle herded and tended in this picturesque setting by fifty-odd *vaqueros* of astonishing skill and character. So attractive was the rancho and its cows, so delightful was the climate of California, that an early Yankee adventurer decided to take the land and cattle away from the "greasers" without due process of law. This Yankee was blessed with the much more convenient if much less florid name of Skaggs.

Don Madariago caused all his stock to be branded thus: ⌒⋀⋀╲ . The *ranchero* liked his brand because its curves were in harmony with his love of adornment in all of life, because it was easy to distinguish from the brands of other ranchers, so that ownership of straying cattle would never be confused, and because it pictured his beloved plush hills. On the side (not the hip) of each of his cows he thus sketched a landscape with a fiery pencil. He called his ranch and brand *Vista Amada,* because the brand did indeed depict, however crudely, a Beloved View.

The Yankee Skaggs did not quietly slip around the edges of the Spaniard's herd and take a half dozen or a dozen of the calves at a time. Instead, he hired four riders to help him—men equally devoid of scruples in the matter—cut through Don Madariago's herd one night and drove off more than a thousand animals. Then the five thieves set in to improve on Don Madariago's subtle artistry.

Under different conditions and in a more American land, they might have succeeded. There in Spanish California, though, they relied on the foolish belief that the Spanish and Mexicans were a submissive people, that one Yankee could whip a dozen greasers any day. (A lot of southwesterners still hold this attitude.) They were caught at their act of re-branding, and in spite of their guns and personal ferocity all five of the men were brought before Don Madariago who rose to meet them in terrible wrath. He took them to the *alcalde*, thence to the *comandante* of the nearest military garrison who owed much of his salary and position to Don Madariago's political influence.

As a Christian act a venerable priest volunteered to serve as defense for the gringos on trial, and he did plead conscientiously for them.

"Possibly, Don Madariago, my son," he said, "the Americans actually needed the cattle they preempted. When one is driven by hunger, the laws of man—"

Don Madariago interrupted him, roaring magnificently.

"No! Need the cows? Hah! One, two cows they need for food maybe, but not a thousand, padre. I have many cows. I would have given them a thousand cows to start a rancho of their own if they had but asked it. But, padre, it is the insult that is unforgivable. Those men—por Dios!—*they* make a frog of my brand!"

The honorable court understood thoroughly. Next dawn the thieves were placed against a church wall and executed by a firing squad while their counsel and confessor held up a cross and uttered last prayers. Here is the frog they had burned with running iron over Don Madariago's three hills:

A great deal of fiction has centered around cattle rustling. Some of it has been written with classic skill but most of it has been the cheapest sort of mass-production, published in the cheapest sort of books and magazines. As a result, conscientious modern scholars (who unfortunately have never been far beyond the doors of the university library) have written theses and delivered addresses decrying the Wild West fiction as lamentable exaggeration and nothing else. Rustling and brand changing and all the drama incident thereto, these scholars contend, simply did not happen in reality. Narratives by bewhiskered old-timers are called grandfather romanticisms, and even the histories are believed tainted by what we should like to imagine was true.

The scholars are as blameworthy as the fictioneers. More so, because the fictioneers claimed only to be writing fiction, worked under no banner of profundity and truth, admittedly were endeavoring merely to entertain. The scholars were hoping to shape seriously the thoughts of mankind, but were themselves in sad error.

Actually, yesterday's cattle rustling *was* sensational. Brand changing *was* a studied art. The brand blotter or rewrite man *really* was a first-class villain with infinite bravado and ingenuity, and he performed notoriously all over the western stage. If he gave rise to many a yarn and story, so be it; we moderns might as well deny the existence of savage Indians in history as say that the cattle rustler was merely a creature of imaginative minds.

It would be difficult indeed for us to exaggerate in telling stories of cattle rustlers. The three true accounts above are but representative of thousands; they are not even the best of the lot, but are among the simpler ones. Old documents, old histories, and the minds of pioneer women and men, now old, can give abundant proof that cattle rustling episodes often caused prolonged feuds and "wars" in the wilder range country. Bands of criminals could organize then as effectively as the gangs of modern crime. Sometimes by sheer strength of men and guns the rustlers forced recognition of the brand they were using for

a blot-over, daring their victimized ranchers to offer any pro-
tests. More often, in such show of strength, several decent
ranch outfits would combine to ride down the rustlers and be
rid of them. Either process was not only expensive, it was
fraught also with adventure, danger, and death.

Or if you would go to more official sources for your proofs,
you have but to dig into the vaults of courthouses in Texas,
New Mexico, Arizona, Oklahoma, or practically any western
state. Take down an old file dated, say, 1870 to 1890. Blow off
the half century of dust. Handle the pages carefully lest you
tear them, for they are more precious than they appear to be.
Look over there on page seventy-odd at the case of the Territory of So-and-So versus Wm. A. Quait, alias Red Bill, Tom
Dunkerly, Fabens McCord, Juan Castellano, Oscar Dabney,
and Indian Mike.

From this record of court proceedings you will learn that the
aforenamed six men terrorized three counties. In their trail they
left dozens of murders. They were guilty of arson, even of
rape. They defied every known law and officer of the law.
They lived and prospered by thievery, and because cattle were
the principal assets which could be stolen, mostly they stole
cows.

One of them, cunning Mr. Fabens McCord, maintained a
front of respectability, lived openly in a big ranch home,
dressed grandly and bribed his way through political and social
life, kept his black henchmen at work behind him all the while.
Everybody knew it but nobody could stop it. (Didn't everybody know Al Capone was a gangster chief in the 1920's? Will
future scholars say that accounts of his exploits are just exaggerated fiction?)

You will learn that the McCord band had many pitched gun

battles and many individual gunning sprees, losing some of their men at times and hiring some more. You will learn that they had half a dozen brands registered under various ownership names, brands that had been ingeniously worked out so that they could be burned over the brands of two or three respectable ranchers. They stole a great many mavericks and young calves and branded them "clean"—not a rewrite job but a first brand—and according to the unwritten law of the range the rightful owners could find no recourse. But as much as possible too they just roped any valuable looking animal, somersaulted it near the fire and marked over the true owner's brand.

Often they would use a wet blanket on the cow, branding with an extra hot iron right through this thick wet cloth. In the hands of an expert this burning process can trace over old brand marks so as to make them look very fresh indeed, and thus minimize chance of detection. Experts among the decent people, however, could detect telltale marks even when the steaming process had been employed. And always it was possible to kill a cow and inspect the branded-over hide from the inside—an almost infallible, but costly, means of proving a case against a rustler.

You will learn that Fabens McCord could slip an occasional thousand dollars to the presiding judge or sheriff and so establish that the poor hard-working McCord band were in reality just "misunderstood", just the victims of prejudice and malicious talk. (Haven't we comparable instances of court corruption in this modern era?) Or, if the people did indignantly elect a sheriff who was conscientious, he would be mysteriously slain, or face unsurmountable perjured evidence that had been bought in advance of any trial.

Study of the old record will reveal that the McCord criminals

held the stage for perhaps four, five, or ten years, but that ultimately—as it always will—decent society became nauseated
with them and vomited them forever out of itself. Law-abiding
ranchers one week just assembled in common indignation, let
their normally hard ranch work go untended, unslung their
rifles and went at this more urgent job. Sheriffs and deputies
and such trappings of organized law were temporarily forgotten. Elderly Mr. Charles Grantham, the quiet old gentleman who had long been running the Five Bar Five brand, was
elected leader and he accepted the job.

"There's nearly a hundred of us," he said then, from his
saddle. "You have guns. Bring in every McCord you can catch
alive. Shoot first, and don't ask questions. Don't leave any
except the dead ones."

It was the longest speech Uncle Charlie had ever made. He
spoke gravely, nodded and spurred his horse. Fifteen days
later, on his front porch there, he was again presiding at the
trial of Wm. A. Quait, alias Red Bill, Tom Dunkerly, Fabens
McCord, Juan Castellano, Oscar Dabney and Indian Mike,
these six being all physically able to stand any sort of earthly
trial when the man roundup was over.

Uncle Charlie Grantham saw to it that the trial was just and
fair, and legal. For instance, he saw to it that the presiding
judge "resigned" rather hastily, and that the Governor of the
Territory appointed him judge. Other necessary officials of
organized law were then and there inducted into office by their
various means, the entire process taking but a few days. Court
was convened immediately. The six defendants sat chained on
a log in the front yard. (Your court recorder has even mentioned that descriptive fact, in the now musty records.) The
officials were sedate, serious. The several hundred spectators

all were armed, and any sympathizers of the McCord band were conspicuously quiet or absent. The trial opened at 9 A.M., and at 3 P.M. the six defendants were swinging from a giant cotton-wood tree. By sundown they had been hauled off and buried and by night the assembled citizens were making righteous merriment against the morrow when they would have to go back home and resume their normal affairs.

The above instance would be notable in that it all was done with due process of law. Many a similar case ended even more quickly; the posse didn't bother to make it legal, they just dispensed justice and went on home. It is, in fact, almost trite now to mention what happened to cattle rustlers captured in the Old West.

As to the exact way in which a rustler would change a rancher's cattle brand, you must realize that each case offered its own problem. The rancher's task was to create a brand which could not be changed easily. The rustler's task was to devise a clever means of changing it anyway. The ingenuity on both sides has been notable.

Obviously the simpler brands offered the easiest changing. The LP was made into a coffee pot: **LP**   It could be made into the Box R, or Box B, or PUP or any of several other designs. These would be almost childish efforts, and yet they have all been used in actual branding and rebranding. So was the Backward Seven thus changed into the Rail A:

The brand of an old-time ranch was known as the H L Connected, like this: **H L**. Immediately after a spring roundup and branding spree, the unscrupulous ranch foreman quietly slipped back to the animals and rebranded hundreds of them with a brand registered in his own name. Because both brands were fresh, his was entirely convincing when the scab formed and dropped off, and so he escaped detection for a long while. His brand was T H E, made this way from that of his boss: ⱧⱧ .

The Bar T brand T̄ has been changed by rustlers into the Curry Comb ⊤̿ . The Eleven Half Circle ⎍ has been changed to the Rocking Chair ⊓ . The Lazy M Ƨ has been changed to the Twin Diamonds ⧓ .

One of the best known tales of rancher versus rustler in brand changing is probably not true, but is at least illustrative. The rancher's brand, so the story goes, was IC. The rustler thought he would be cute, so he stole IC cows and rebranded them to read ICU. But the rancher went him one cuter, drove back his own cows and as a significant warning added one letter to the brand to make it read: ICU2.

An even more famous brand changing story is that of the big Ten-in-Texas ranch. For a long time everybody thought this ranch's brand was proof against rustlers. It was XIT, and nobody could devise a satisfactory alteration. Even today, because of the story, cowboys often pass the time away by drawing in the dust, trying to make a convincing re-design. In time a clever rustler did start changing the XIT and was haled into court. His design was so clever that the jury acquitted him, accepting his plea that it couldn't be made from XIT. He was said to have been paid five thousand dollars afterward to show how he did it, and to stop doing it to XIT cows. You may already know the story, but if you don't you can have your fun trying to figure out a changed design of your own. Then turn to page 136 and see what the rustler did.

The "cold" brand—more accurately, the hair brand—would be applied by rustlers on occasions, or by cowboys who were thieving a little on the side. This was done by pressing the iron on quickly through a wet blanket, or by lightly touching the animal's hair. In either case the immediate appearance was of a permanent scar, but within a few weeks the hair would grow out and the marks disappear. Then the dishonest man could re-brand to suit himself without fear of detection by brand inspectors.

Decoy brands—small, unobtrusive marks of ownership burned on an animal's underside—sometimes were used by ranch owners to trap rustlers. Choicest calves or steers were used, and they would be left unbranded otherwise. The ruse seldom worked, however, because the rustler usually was just as shrewd as the honest man, or more so.

Because it was so easy geometrically to change many brands, the ranchers realized many years ago that they must unite to combat rustlers. Rustlers were a problem even before the practice of registering brands was started. Before brands were registered, what was to prevent a man ten or fifteen miles away from adopting your brand and swearing it was also his own? He could steal your cattle and prove ownership, and your only recourse would be to steal yours back—and perhaps some of his for good measure. True, custom or unspoken law tended to make brands exclusive in a given region, but boundaries were vague and customs subject to "convenient" interpretations. Or even if the man didn't have your exact brand, he could rewrite one of his own.

The result was that cattlemen's associations came into existence, and brand inspectors were hired by them. The Colorado Cattlemen's Association was organized as early as 1869, for instance. Other states soon followed, and today practically every western state has its organization of ranchers which may wield strong political and social pressure as well as protect interests in such things as brands. These groups have caused the state government to maintain official registries to avoid brand duplications, have forced police action against thieves in many cases, have published handbooks giving names and addresses of brands currently used, have seen to it that the brand inspectors are efficient at their jobs.

The brand inspector has inevitably emerged as the detective of rangeland fiction, and that's precisely what he is in fact, too. He must keep ever alert for the brand that has been blotted out and replaced by a new one. He must have a critical eye for the rewritten brand. He must pounce on rustlers who will sometimes be as clever as sin, collecting evidence with which to convict them and seeing that they are imprisoned. If the case of thievery happens to be particularly flagrant, he must act as intermediary between his own bosses and the established agencies of law, to forestall possible lynching as in the olden days.

Some of these inspectors develop a truly remarkable memory for cattle brands, holding thousands of them in mind and calling them off at will when riding through a great herd of animals at roundup, or spotting them in the pens at shipping and receiving points. Their services are excellent, for further instance, in counting animals as well as in identification. Modern mechanical counting devices are said to be no more accurate than some of the more skilled brand inspectors, who can "tally" a big herd and remember exactly how many animals were carrying each of perhaps twenty or thirty brands.

2.

The Old West, many people will tell you, is now dead and gone forever. The Indian is at the end of his trail. The cowboy has become nothing more than a motion picture actor. The cattle rustler is but a picturesque villain of yesteryear, if admitted at all.

Such profound lamentations are generalities which seem important but which simply aren't true. To be sure, we no longer travel in exactly the same kind of stagecoaches that our grandfathers knew, nor wear the same kind of clothing nor shoot the same kind of guns. But consider these statistical facts: Lo, the poor Red Man, having achieved both governmental and sentimental bounty, and never having heard of Margaret Sanger, is breeding more and more little Indians every day so that his race is definitely increasing; more American consumers are eating much more beef than in the wild western days, and since beef can be raised only by cowboys, these saddle-settin' fellows can hardly be called vanishing; finally, in keeping with everything else in this swiftly-moving era, cattle rustling itself has become streamlined.

During the past few years cattlemen's associations throughout the West have repeatedly listed rustling as a problem second only to that of market price fluctuations. In 1939 *more range cattle were being stolen than at any other time in history!*

Here is a highly significant headline from the leading newspaper in a western state:

CATTLE MEN OF COLORADO CONSIDER
'SECRET THREE' TO FIGHT RUSTLERS

It might have been a newsy headline in 1875 and would have fitted in with the times. But it was published on February 14, 1936.

Another headline, over a news article dated Denver, Colorado, October 2, 1938, read:

RANCHERS FIGHT COW 'RUSTLERS'

Look For Way To Put Branding Marks
On Bills Of Sale Just As They
Are Burned On Animals' Sides

Both articles were Associated Press wire releases, and were displayed prominently in practically every daily paper in the West and to a lesser extent throughout the East.

On August 1, 1938, a headline over an article from Nogales, Arizona, said:

CATTLE THEFT RING FOUGHT

Ranchers of Sonora Organize
To Combat Wholesale Rustling

"Cattle rustling on a scale never approached in the most lawless days of the American west is now going on in the Mexican State of Sonora," the article announced, "and Mexican officers have come here to seek co-operation of the United States Border Patrol and other American officials in breaking up an elaborately organized syndicate believed to head in high places. The Mexican officers estimate that Sonora ranchers alone lose five thousand animals a month. Many of these are driven secretly to Phoenix and Los Angeles stock yards. At least one hundred cowboys are in the theft syndicate's employ. Financial backers and 'brains' of the syndicate, the Mexican officials state, are moneyed men of Arizona and Sonora."

From Cheyenne, Wyoming, on February 1, 1939, came a United Press article headlined:

WEST AROUSED BY EFFICIENT HERD RUSTLERS

Ranchers Call for United Action
By States to Curb Menace

The article stated that the Wyoming Stock Growers Association was urging similar associations in every other state to join it in a united militant effort. "Rustling nowadays differs from the old-time raiding only in the efficiency of the modern thieves," the Association officers were quoted. "Authorities have found it virtually impossible to capture the bandits and, when captured, to convict them. Many large ranches have revived the old system of 'riding herd' over the cattle, but on scattered rangelands this proves ineffectual. Threats of bringing back King Colt and the noose have been expressed by cattlemen most heavily damaged."

Now, exactly how does the modern streamlined cattle rustler operate? Best way to answer is to present, again, some actual scenes and episodes from the modern rustler-rancher war.

Across the colorful Southwest are several broad highways linking coast with coast and carrying on their smooth pavement many thousands of trucks and passenger automobiles. Unlike the East, it has a sparse population. A city or town or village will appear mirage-like on the horizon, move toward you, the traveler, and present a sudden teem and work of humanity in the urban pattern, then vanish from your rear-view mirror as quickly as it appeared in the windshield. In retrospect it will seem like a lost thing in the vast wilderness surrounding. For miles and miles and miles not even a filling station will show other evidence of man. Binoculars might reveal an occasional

ranch house in some far canyon or field, and sometimes a windmill will catch the sun's glint and shoot it back from ten miles
away. But mostly the landscape is one of sahuaros and yuccas
and prickly pears and ironwoods and palos verdes, and boulders
and mountains splashed with purple and crimson and gold. The
highway will split and signs will say 86 miles to here and 120
to there. A crude sign at a dirt turnoff will have been "painted"
with a hot iron, reading V–/ 8 .

You may or may not know that the V Bar Slash ranch house
is eight miles down that trail, or that the steers which amble con-
trarily across the highway—endangering your life and infuri-
ating you as you skid your wheels—are V Bar Slash steers.
Every few miles on the smooth pavement you will see a dead
jackrabbit, run over and crushed by a car that blinded it in the
previous night, and buzzards will rise flappily to let you pass.
Frequently, too, the dead animal will be a four-foot rattlesnake,
and mayhap yours will even be the privilege of running over
the live snake so that you can get out and cut off its rattles for
souvenirs. You will have to pull off to the shoulder and stop
along here somewhere (surely so, if you have children in your
car!) to commune with Nature, and after the physical communion will come communion of the soul. The incomparable
lift that comes from isolation, from height, from wild distances,
will be yours there in just a few minutes as you silently stare.
You will marvel that there is another living human being or
family anywhere in all the world, although of course you are
but two hours or so from the next town, and you can see fifty
or sixty steers resting down yonder in the arroyo in the shade of
mesquite trees. Such is precisely the setting that the modern
cattle rustler loves.

In a setting like this, on a morning last May, a huge motor

truck of the furniture van type pulled to the side of the highway. Two men rode in the cab. When the van stopped, one man entered the big tonneau from the front while the other went behind and, surprisingly, let down a heavy hinged door. The door then slanted right down to the ground to make a runway. Down this runway the man inside led two saddled horses. Both men mounted and rode toward the fifty or sixty resting steers.

The steers were docile enough. In less than two minutes one of them had been lassoed and was being hazed toward the truck. With the skill of practice the men pulled and drove it right up the runway into the van, snapped a chain across the rear and went for another animal.

The men were both expert ropers. They made no fuss nor hullabaloo, they just slipped into the herd, edged out the selected animal and conducted it right up the slope into their van. This process was repeated ten times in not more than forty minutes, and by that time the van was almost full. There was just room to squeeze in the two saddled horses, and when they were in the drop door was lifted and locked again, and the truck was soon on its way.

The side of the truck bore a sign: INDEPENDENT TRANSFER COMPANY. MOVING. STORAGE. It appeared innocuous enough. Certainly it showed nothing suspicious. It was like any of hundreds of freight trucks to be seen on the highways every night or day.

This truck moved on at reasonably fast speed for more than two hundred miles. That meant it had passed through two or three counties. At about 5 P.M. it turned from the highway at the edge of a city, took a side road and presently drew up at the gate of a packing plant. A foreman came to meet it.

"Got some good fat stuff here," the driver told the foreman.
"Ten head."

"Drive under the big shed," the foreman ordered.

Under the big shed the ponies and then the ten steers were released. The ponies were watered by one man, put back in the truck and fed. The foreman appraised the steers critically. He didn't need to weigh them because he was an experienced man.

"Three hundred dollars," said the foreman. It was a price about thirty percent under the current market price for such animals on foot, but the other man didn't argue. Both of them knew the circumstances. The truck man had no secure ground on which to stand, although there is a law against receiving stolen property.

"All right," he said.

The foreman went inside and came back with three hundred dollars in cash, and the truckers drove away. They had a goodly sum to split for their day's work. They could deliver another load, from the same or some similar ranch, once or twice more that week if they wanted to. They could keep it up all year, making a net income of better than ten thousand dollars. With that much they could have nice homes and travel to all the World's Fairs and send their daughters off to finishing school and their sons to U. S. C. or Stanford so they would grow up to be intelligent American citizens.

Meanwhile, the foreman would have put the ten steers promptly through the butchering process, and likely as not the two truckers' families ate some of that same beef within a few days, having bought it over the counter of local grocers. The foreman's profit may have come either of two ways: through selling the steers to his own boss at the established market price and pocketing the thirty percent difference, or by being in connivance with the boss himself.

From this it must not be concluded that all or even most of the packing houses are dishonest, or even that most of the foremen are. But unquestionably enough of them do receive stolen animals to make big profits at it, and they have a dozen or more ways in which to appear innocent and beyond the reach of the law.

Suppose an inspector had come into the packing plant that night. How could he suspect anything when the stolen animals were just ten of a hundred carcasses receiving routine handling? Suppose anybody—say even a conscientious packing house employe—had seen the ten steers branded V Bar Slash before they were killed that night. Wouldn't they have aroused suspicions? No, because they would have been a mere part of a big bawling, odoriferous herd waiting there to be slain. Many brands would have been represented among them. If by chance curiosity someone had investigated the records for these particular ten V Bar Slash steers, he would have found them duly entered on the books, and even a receipt for the money paid for them. How could anyone know the receipt was not entirely accurate, was in truth forged?

The chances are perhaps a hundred to one that the V Bar Slash owner would never miss his ten steers. No big rancher ever knows exactly how many cattle he owns because the animals roam far and wide, dodge cowboys during roundup, have calves in singles and sometimes in twins, die off naturally. Ten or a hundred might never be missed at all. But suppose the V Bar Slash owner *did* discover his loss. What could he do? Telephone or ride in to the sheriff, surely, but the sheriff would be impotent in the matter.

"Waal, Mistuh Wascom, I'll shore try to do what I can," the sheriff would say, earnestly, "but I don't rightly know where to turn. I only got six deppities, suh, and as you know, our county's bigger'n most eastern states. We just couldn't stand guard over every man's ranch all th' time, suh. And it's no tellin' when ner whar them steers was took, now."

The truth of that would be too apparent. Even the rancher would recognize it. He and his cowboys might, by careful search, find the spot where the big truck stopped, see even the tracks where steers were caught and loaded. But that was a week ago or day before yesterday at best, and the truck could be a thousand miles away by now.

If, by extremely remote chance (rustlers are always vigilant) a wandering V Bar Slash cowboy or two had suddenly topped a nearby hill and seen the rustlers loading the cows, there might have been a snappy gun battle, but most likely not. The rustlers would have shunted their own horses quickly into the van, closed the drop door and sped away at sixty miles an hour. Down the road a few miles they would have kicked out the stolen cows, hence if the cowboys had contrived to phone ahead and have the men arrested (very unlikely) the van would hold no incriminating evidence. Even the side boards bearing the signs would have been changed presently, and license plates from another state bolted on.

Assuming that the rustlers got away with their loot, suppose now that they did happen to cross a county with a particularly vigilant sheriff, whose deputies had orders to inspect all trucks.

"Halt!" a deputy would command the thieves. "I'll have to see what you got there, men."

"Why, it's just some young steers, officer," the truckers

would say. "Some we bought to take to our ranch and feed up for market this fall."

"You got a bill of sale?"

"Shore have."

"Lemme see it."

The bill of sale looks all right. It declares in plain language that W. D. Wascom, owner of the V Bar Slash ranch, has hereby received payment in full for ten Hereford steers branded V Bar Slash on the left side, and has delivered said steers to known agents for Webb Lee of the Lee's Forked Lightning ranch. It is signed by W. D. Wascom himself. In the deputy's car are books showing the brands registered in his and surrounding states. He thumbs down the alphabetical list of names. Yep, he finds W. D. Wascom, V Bar Slash, swallow fork in right ear. That checks with the steers in the truck. He also finds Webb Lee's Forked Lightning brand. He glances again at the two men in the truck; they look like nothing but old tanned cowpunchers, sitting up there now calmly rolling cigarettes. They catch his eye and hold out the makin's to him. Shucks, everything's okay.

"Well, all right fellers," the deputy says. "Just had to check up, accordin' to orders. So long."

"Sure! Sure, sheriff, and much obliged. So long." And so they roll on down the highway.

Forged bills of sale, forged orders and credentials of every sort are likely to be carried by the motorized rustlers, although it is rare indeed that they need them. Not all of the truckers work as in the instance described above; sometimes fewer steers are hauled at one load, and sometimes the steers are shot, butchered and loaded into refrigerated trucks right there in the wilds. Immediate butchering lessens danger from the possible telltale brand marks on hide, and the valuable meat can be sold at reduced price to any of several wholesalers or canners who don't care where their merchandise originates. Great sides of beef can be unloaded quickly at night, stamped with an "official" government seal and number, and turn up on respectable retailers' counters by the following afternoon. Hotel men, restaurateurs, boarding houses, offer standing markets for cheap beef brought to them quietly. No questions are likely to be asked if the meat is plainly of good quality and in good condition, and the price is conspicuously down. There are laws about inspections and all that sort of thing, to be sure, but when hands are bloody and work is pressing from a dozen sources, the back-alley sale is likely to be consummated with scant formality. Just bring the meat in and hang it in the refrigerator room, and here's your money.

Up to 1939, state governments had simply ignored the existence of motorized cattle rustling—with a few instances in exception. Sporadic mention of it was heard. Some bills had been introduced in legislatures, governors had orated about it in campaigning, but little had been done, for the simple reason that no definite plan for combating rustlers had been offered. Adequate policing seemed to be prohibitive in cost, even if an effective method had been offered, which hadn't. In 1937 and again in 1939 cattlemen's associations brought sufficient pressure to bear on their Congressmen to get a federal anti-rustling law passed, but President Roosevelt both times refused to sign it.[1]

[1] This cattle theft bill, President Roosevelt argued, would extend federal police jurisdiction over offenses of the petty larceny type, thus encroaching on the police power of several states and moving the federal government out of its proper sphere. His argument has some merit, but it leaves the cattle rustling problem unsolved.

At this writing many association officials feel that federal control will be the ultimate answer, to be started in 1940 or later. Conceivably Uncle Sam can do what the individual counties and states apparently can not. Maybe his "G-Men" can don western hats and six-shooters and become a picturesque agency for putting cattle thieving at an end. Certainly something will have to be done to bring the force of law and order up to the efficiency of the streamlined rustlers themselves. Organized, motorized thieves nowadays put to shame the saddled rustler of yesteryear, whose chief pride and skill was in rewriting somebody else's brand.

CHAPTER IX

DISTINGUISHED BRANDS

Both the heraldry of Europe and the heraldry of the range-land have been lifted to a distinction by a relatively few men who acquired power and fame, and as history still sings of those few armored knights who rose above the commonplace, so will Americans talk for all time about the greatest cattle ranches and brands. Obviously only a representative few of the distinguished brands and famous cattle kings can be mentioned here, and it is with genuine regret that the authors omit so many. Complete coverage would require not a whole book but a whole library.

If greatness be measured in terms of economic, political, social and moral strength, then the greatest cattle rancher who ever lived was not an American but a Mexican named Luis Terrazas whose *four hundred thousand* cattle carried this brand:

Certainly no man on this continent, and probably no other man anywhere except some dictator or king, has ever owned outright so many thousands of cattle at one time. The rancho of Don Luis Terrazas also was probably the largest privately owned ranch ever known. It was larger than many a kingdom. A horseman could ride in any given direction for weeks and not travel across it. It extended from Juárez, Chihuahua, which is just across the Rio Grande from El Paso, Texas, all the way to Chihuahua City, a distance of more than two hundred miles.

The area was approximately six million acres. *One* acre is equal to five and a half baseball diamonds; all of Manhattan Island is less than fifteen thousand acres.

Five magnificent haciendas were built on the Terrazas *rancho grande*, and the imaginative tales concerning society in these homes are surpassed only by the facts in the matter. Where Don Luis lived, lived grandeur indeed; not ostentation, but genuine grandeur, the sort made worthy by dignity and restraint. The old don himself dressed in the highly colorful costumes of Spain and those around him did likewise. The handsomest *caballeros* and the loveliest *señoritas* adorned porches and patios of the Terrazas homes. Mexico's foremost painters and sculptors and authors gathered there, and the best recommendation a Mexican musician could have was the privilege of saying that he had performed in concert for Don Luis and his friends. No gayer, more colorful fiestas ever were staged than those under Terrazas' patronage; sometimes the dancing and eating and cockfighting and rodeo contests and lovemaking would continue for weeks.

Americans stood in awe of the old don and any day he visited across the line in El Paso was epochal. It is told that an American cattle buyer went down to visit him and was impressed by the fatness and generally good condition of his stock. But the American did not know the extent of the don's holdings.

"I'd like to buy some of your cows, Don Luis," the guest offered. "Could you let me have as many as four thousand head of three-year-olds?"

Don Luis smiled graciously. "Four thousand, señor? Certainly. What color would you prefer?"

So wealthy a man and one so important socially of course held political influence, too. But alas, the political history of

Mexico has been one long game of chance. Whether he had wanted to or not, Don Luis had to take sides, as everybody must in Mexico. When Porfirio Diaz was in the ascendancy he gave military protection to the grand don of Chihuahua, allowing him virtually to run that vast state. When revolution came and Diaz was ousted, Terrazas and his sons had to flee for their lives and the Terrazas glory ended forever. The grand ranch houses were mostly destroyed; the acreage was cut up; the cattle confiscated. Don Luis himself died in the United States in 1923.

He and his magnificence are symbolic of an old order lost now even from Mexico—which like its neighbor republic to the north is trying to go ultra-modern—but memories of Don Luis will live a long time. Cowboys throughout the Southwest, on both sides the border, still argue about the meaning of his brand, which could be called the T H S but which was not that in Don Luis' mind. It was simply a combination of lines and curves pleasing in his eyes, and it had no satisfactory translation regardless of the fame it achieved. It was merely the Terrazas brand.

The "King Kingdom" is the largest ranch on this continent today. It is fittingly located in the largest state, and the one which has always had the most range cattle. It functions as a grand monument to the industry, and to confound the cloistered lecturers who persist in saying that big cattle ranches are all gone.

A gentleman named Robert E. Lee was stationed with the United States cavalry in Brownsville, Texas, some years before the Civil War, and he chanced to form a friendship with a steamboat pilot named Richard King. Both the young men, like most others of that era, were looking for new geographic

and business horizons. Lee seemed destined to have a career as
a soldier, and subsequent events proved indeed what his claim to
fame should be. But Richard King saw prosperity in the cattle
business.

South Texas then was just boundless, open land. The great
coastal plain extended inland for many miles, was blessed with
a mild climate, a few streams, rich browse and grass. Labor was
cheap. Cattle raising was a picturesque masculine enterprise.
Richard King thought he might wisely take a chance in spite of
the salient fact that savage Indians and Mexican bandits had
been and still were a menace. He bought the Santa Gertrudis
lands in 1851, married a girl named Henrietta Chamberlin, and
with her built up the most valuable American ranch property
of all time.

King died in 1885. Mrs. King died in 1925 when past ninety
years of age, and by this time the original Santa Gertrudis property had swelled to almost unbelievable proportions. Mrs.
Robert J. Kleberg, daughter of the founders, was spiritual head
after her mother's death although management had been willed
to a group of six trustees. Youngest of the six, Robert Justus
Kleberg, Jr., grandson of the founder, was elected executive
director and by 1939 he and his associates had still further in-
creased the ranch holdings of land, cattle and other property.
Today the "King Kingdom" embraces approximately a million
and a half acres lying between Corpus Christi and Brownsville.
To envision so vast a property in modern days is difficult for the
average city resident. One acre is enough to be extremely valuable under certain conditions. All of Delaware is no larger than
the King Ranch.

The ranch is so vast that the ruins of a village were found in
one part of it only a few years ago, never having been discov-

ered before. There is a full month's difference in climate between the northern edge and the southern edge of the King land, and ranch cars all carry compasses lest travelers become lost. The ranch has seventeen hundred miles of fence, costing almost four hundred dollars a mile. It divides the property into one hundred and thirty-five pastures, some containing as much as twelve square miles each and the smallest having six thousand acres.

The ranch has streams, but not nearly enough, so to combat drouth the owners have dug more than three hundred and fifty wells. Many of them are artesian but a majority are pumped by windmills and some by gasoline pumps. Five crews of men with specially equipped trucks spend all their time servicing the pumps and windmills. Literally millions of dollars have been spent also for horses, saddles, bridles, guns, automobiles, trucks, houses—("Santa Gertrudis," the ranch headquarters, is a veritable mansion)—railroads, highways, land-clearing machinery, all the other limitless necessities for such a vast enterprise. Inheritance tax alone, at the death of the founder's widow in 1925, exceeded a million dollars, and there is no adequate way of appraising the total value of the property today.

The average number of cattle grazing on the King ranch is about a hundred and thirty thousand head. Originally the herd started with Texas Longhorns. These were replaced in time by the meatier, more valuable English breeds, especially the Herefords, and in recent years a distinctly new breed of its own has been developed on the great ranch by crossing shorthorns and Brahmas.

It is only natural that the King Ranch should be a powerful political and social force in Texas. Men and women bearing the King name, or the in-law name of Kleberg, are better known nationally than most of the Texas governors, and frequently are persons of more force and influence. Distinguished Americans often visit the ranch to hunt and rest or watch the activities there. The homes and corrals and ranges are like spectacular western movie sets. Everybody dresses in broad Stetsons, colored shirts, "levis" (blue denim pants), leather chaps and boots and spurs, not just to show off but because the costume is both pleasing and practical there. Guests on the ranch are similarly outfitted soon after arrival. The dining table in the headquarters home has places for fifty, and practically every meal sees twenty or more persons seated. Homefolks and guests may eat at any hour they choose, selecting from the best of American or Mexican dishes.

Most physical work of the ranch is done not by American cowboys but by their Mexican counterparts called *vaqueros*. (Vah-KAY-ros, from which comes, by mispronunciation, our range word "buckaroo".) Some three hundred and fifty of these Mexican men and boys are regularly at work converting King grass into King beef, shipping King beef to market. They ride the finest horses money can buy or skill can breed, for the King men have not only developed a distinguished breed of steer, they have produced fine new strains of horse flesh as well. These Mexicans are far superior to the peon or greaser lot of poor workmen too common in Southwest Texas. They are a high order, who make careers of serving the King ranch owners. Besides the *vaqueros* there are a hundred or so other Mexican families whose men, women and children are devoted servants and workers. "Bad blood" among them all has been weeded out and is kept out so that the King employees are a closed clan justly proud of their clanship. It is told, by way of illustration, that a curious man entered heaven and saw several Mexicans who although obviously sinless were tied to posts. A Running W of gold on each of their halos didn't explain anything to the curious one, so he finally asked good St. Peter why the Mexicans were tied there. "If we did not tie them," St. Peter replied, "they would depart immediately for the King ranch."

Nobody now seems to know for sure just why Richard King chose the Running W for his brand. Through the decades it has adorned hundreds of thousands of cows, and still is the coat of arms worn by the animals that go to northern markets each year in dozens of trainloads. The brand is simply an extended, slightly leaning letter W, like this: $\mathcal{W}$. Because of its pictorial suggestion the King Mexicans have long referred to it as the Little Snake.

The significance of this brand and of brands in general is adequately attested in the true story of the King foreman who had a little difficulty in the old days. The year was 1884, and Walt Billingsley was in charge of the hands driving a King herd from South Texas to Cheyenne, Wyoming. Everything moved smoothly until the herd and drivers bedded down one night outside a Nebraska town. Mr. Billingsley kindly let a group of the boys go into town after dark for a little relaxation, but cautioned them to come back well before dawn. Six of them hadn't shown up when the sun rose. Mr. Billingsley rode in and found them.

"You're every one fired right here and now," he told them emphatically. "I owe you better'n a hundred dollars each. Come on over to the bank."

They trudged solemnly behind him, feeling their disgrace but powerless to avoid it. They waited outside while the boss went to the cashier.

"Sorry, but you're strangers to me," the cautious banker

declared. "I can't cash any check or lend you any money unless you're identified. You say you're from the King Ranch. Can anybody here identify you? Have any proof at all?"

Mr. Billingsley's anger, already pretty well boiled up, now boiled plumb over. Muttering, he rode back to the edge of town, barked some orders, and led a strange parade back right down Main Street to the bank. The dust was all-encompassing, the bawling and snorting of cows was magnificent in its way. Mr. Billingsley dismounted at the bank and again went inside.

"Come out here," he told the cashier. "There's ten thousand cows with a Runnin' W burned onto their sides, and a hundred and fifty horses with it. Now come 'ere"—he pulled the dressed-up banker right out into the dust cloud—"this here's th' chuck-wagon, and you c'n see thet Runnin' W on its side. Thet mule th' cook's ridin' is branded with King's brand, and so is th' saddle on him. In th' wagon here is some left over pies —see, here is a Runnin' W forked and cooked onto th' crust of every one of them. Now we'll look at th' saddles which th' men are—"

"Never mind! Never mind!" pleaded the banker. "Come on in and get your money, any amount you want. I don't need any better identification."

Even though he was born the first son of a king and so was himself destined to be a king some day, young Edward Windsor showed keen interest in the royal farm in Cornwall. As a boy he would go there and work with the livestock. It may rightly be assumed that he was guarded and sheltered as any princeling must be, but the world of the 1930's will remember that Edward was a man of independent will, not afraid to ignore traditions or to set them. In that he was the ideal "American" cattleman, and it was partly that spirit which led to his purchase in 1919 of a four-thousand-acre ranch on this hemisphere. Doubtless he would have preferred one in the "Wild West"—the North American region which, however vague as to boundaries, holds most of glamor to Englishmen—but the royal conscience dictated that he at least keep in English lands. His acreage lay near Calgary, rightly called the cowboy capital of the Dominion, and it was wild enough to satisfy any imaginative young man.

As often as possible he came to his ranch, threw aside his derby and donned a wide cowboy hat. He could hang the royal dignity on a fence post and shout "YIP-PEEEEEEE!" with the most exuberant cowhand, and if he never developed much skill with a lasso it wasn't because he didn't try. He *might* have been a crackerjack horseman, if his station hadn't demanded that he ride most of the time in the little postage-stamp saddles of high society. A man just can't be a cowboy on Tuesday and a fox-hunting dude on Wednesday. One of the two horses is sure to dump the rider ignominiously over its head, and the world still remembers Prince Edward's embarrassing falls. But even as the world chuckled, it admired Edward for being that occidental character known as a good sport.

The ranch itself of course was not operated to earn anybody a living. Nevertheless efficiency was the keynote there. Prize-winning cattle, horses, and sheep exhibited at Canadian and American shows were evidence of the quality of its purebred stock. It contributed to the industry by serving as an experimental ranch. Edward, surfeited with pink teas, loved to squat on his haunches and discuss the technique of branding; it is not often that a prince can so get down to earthy things, but there is no quicker way to do it than to mingle with cowboys.

Three feathers together, a motto—*Ich Dien*—and the letters

E P, were engraved on the ranch stationery, and the feathers and letters were "engraved" on the ranch animals as well. Three ostrich plumes are a symbol of the Principality of Wales. The crest they make dates back to the fourteenth century. Tradition is that the Black Prince, having slain the blind king of Bohemia at the Battle of Crécy, assumed the Bohemian's feather crest and his motto *Ich Dien,* the latter being the German words meaning *I Serve.* The origin, however, is controversial, and some historians believe the crest to be a rebus of Queen Philippa's hereditary title which was Countess of Ostre Vant (ostrich feather).

The very controversy made the three feathers an ideal brand. It held interest; it got "talked about". It not only adhered to the heraldry of the range, it linked that with the heraldry of Europe.

The Three Feathers brand looked like this:

It could be made with a running iron, but its graceful curves were best stamped on. It was burned on the right shoulder of all the prince's horses, but most of his cows were branded E P on the ribs. These letters meant simply Edward Prince.

Time, however, has seen Edward Prince become king, seen him shock conservative old England by swapping his throne for what he called love, seen him become virtually an outcast from the British heart and home. Time too has seen the virtual disintegration of the E P Ranch and brand.

Many an eastern man has found occasion in the past forty-odd years to travel down to Austin, Texas, and has suddenly discovered—to his invariable amazement—another National Capitol looming there on Congress Avenue.

It does indeed look like the Capitol at Washington at first glance. It is almost as broad, its dome is very similar and almost as high. It is the biggest thing, literally and figuratively, in this otherwise unimportant plains town.[1] And next to the Alamo at San Antonio, which is a sort of shrine, it is the one object dearest to the heart of all Texans. Their pride in it is entirely justified because it is in keeping with the general bigness of their state. It must have appeared somewhat exaggerated when it was constructed in the 1880's, but wisdom of its builders is shown in the fact that it has not yet been outgrown, even though Texas has expanded immeasurably in population and political machinery.

Now when nineteenth century Texans wanted to build this thing, and build for their future, they had grandiose vision but they lacked the money to back it up. The State of Texas owned millions of acres of land, and no cash. Would any financier or contractor care to erect a capitol building in return for, say, a few entire Texas counties? It seemed like a strange invitation, and did indeed stir up some political squabbling. Nevertheless land was *real* estate then as it never has been since; men were still rooted to the soil, a land owner was held to be substantial. So a syndicate of Chicago financiers popped right down and called the Texan bluff.

They built the immense structure of red Texas granite and collected their pay in the form of ten counties in the Panhandle —that squared off top of Texas which sticks up farthest north. The region was almost as wild as it had been when Columbus sailed. It held some scattered white settlements, but the moneyed syndicate knew that it wasn't ready for subdivision as home sites, and that big-scale farming would find no outlet for its

---

[1] Texas University will resent this. But the U is not really a part of Austin, is a definite entity in itself which just happens to center there.

produce there. Unless gold or silver could be discovered on it, the land offered a quick profit only through cattle ranching. Cows could always be driven to market somewhere.

The upshot was that the ten Texas counties comprising about three million acres (remember, this is *two hundred times* as large as Manhattan Island!) was surrounded by fifteen hundred miles of fence to become the largest fenced cattle ranch in history. It was bigger than many a state, bigger than the holdings of many a prince or king who has thought himself immensely wealthy. It was a high plains country gashed by some spectacular canyons. The air was crisp, cool, zestful, even when the summer sun bore down, although winters were likely to be spotted with blizzards. In general the range there was too dry, but to offset the drouth the syndicate erected six hundred windwills.

As rapidly as possible the herds were built up by purchase and by breeding. No heifer which looked good at all was ever spayed or sold at first; she was encouraged to bear a calf every year for ten or twelve years. Grass was bountiful, winter browse was good, and as the work progressed the syndicate acquired other holdings in Montana so that Texas-bred animals were trekked up there to stock that northern rangeland, just as Texas-bred animals spread elsewhere throughout the West in the latter half of that century.

Naturally some forceful men were required to boss a ranch over two hundred miles long, holding a hundred and fifty thousand head of cattle. Just imagine roundup time there! Nowadays, on many ranches, the boys can ride over yonder in the field and down through the back pasture, drive in all the cows and be back in time for supper. Roundup on this Capitol Syndicate's ranch was practically a year-long enterprise. And the man who bossed it and all other of its endeavors from the beginning was Col. B. H. Campbell who had been a prominent cattleman in Indian Territory, to the east. Nobody knew Campbell as Col., or as B. H., however. In his own ranch work he had chosen this brand: $\overline{BQ}$. It reads Bar B Q or, as the cowboys regarded it, Barbecue. And as Barbecue Campbell it became first the nickname and then virtually the only name this gentleman had.

He carried that name with him to the big new Capitol Syndicate Ranch in Texas. The Syndicate ordered Barbecue Campbell to purchase a complete new ranch outfit—cattle, horses, chuck-wagons, saddles, harness, tools, implements, everything. These things had to be marked with ownership. Campbell might not have realized it, but his was the honor of starting a new western legend, a new chapter in range heraldry. He had somehow to contrive a suitable new coat of arms. One of the men he hired was Ab Blocker, known as the best trail driver in Texas, and the two distinguished cow men squatted together.

"Ab, we got to have a brand," Barbecue told him. "What'll it be? I'd say it ought to be something simple, which could be made by the roughest cowboy with a single iron bar, and which would give the rustlers a lot of trouble."

"Yep," Ab admitted. "It ought to be right important looking, too. This here outfit's gonna be big, Barbecue. Now let me figure some."

He began making lines in the sand with his finger, apparently aimless lines, Barbecue looking on.

"This ranch is made of Ten Texas counties—ten in Texas—lemme see, Barbecue," Ab squinted up at him, "don't the letter X stand for ten sometimes?"

"It does."

"Um. Well, how's this, then?" Ab Blocker sketched the following design in the sand:

$$X I \curlyvee$$

"The X I T," Ab explained, "could stand for Ten in Texas. It could be made with a short iron bar, just stamping it on twice for the X, once for the I, and twice for the T. Or you could make stamping irons carrying the whole thing at once. Looks to me like it would be hard to change, too."

Barbecue Campbell stared at it a long time, trying to figure a way for rustlers to change it. He couldn't. The more he stared the more he liked it. He liked its looks—it was simple and distinctive—and he liked the connotation of its initials: Ten in Texas.

"Hell, Ab, that's damn good!" Barbecue finally said. "We'll use it."

And so the XIT brand for the Capitol Syndicate was duly recorded in Potter County, Texas, and in other counties as governments were organized. Exact dates are not on record, but the first two recordings were sometime between 1887 and 1890.

The XIT (called X I T, not "exit") of course became known rapidly. The sheer frequency of it made it an advertisement for the Capitol Syndicate's stock, in addition to advertising the strange circumstance of the Syndicate's entering Texas in the first place. Innumerable legends and stories now exist concerning the XIT ranch, concerning Barbecue Campbell and Ab Blocker and many another capable man of the ranch personnel. Hundreds of cowboys were required to carry on the work of the ranch, and while they were not Mexicans they did have career work there much as the Mexicans did and still do on the King Ranch in South Texas. A good young man could come to the XIT knowing he had a steady job for life if he wanted it, but knowing also that he'd get kicked off the range—perhaps literally—if he proved dishonest or started raising hell. If he grew old in the service he could be gracefully shunted to lighter service than breaking broncos or lassoing steers. One notable wind-up place for a decrepit cowboy is the cook shack, where he can still serve his fellows, still be in on the range talk and comradeship, while keeping his self-respect by earning an honest wage. If his biscuits are hard at first and his pastry leathery, no matter; under relentless gibing from his friends he'll learn.

The sentimental aspects of the XIT were in Texas, but the cold financial aspects were in Chicago. When it became financially expedient to break up the XIT, the breaking-up was begun. Today, the XIT is a fading memory. The herds are gone. The syndicate holds onto a few acres of land, but most of the ten Texas counties have been cut up into farms, small ranches, town sites, lots for homes. Periodically, however, former employes of the ranch get together to swap liquor and tobacco and tales of the old times; you are fortunate indeed if you can manage to sit in on some of their impromptu sessions. Their talk is salty with the lore of rangeland, their words precious in idiom and pronunciation. Invariably these old boys of the XIT Association get around to talking of their beloved brand, and invariably they tell and re-tell the story of the one rustler who made good at stealing their branded cows. He was caught and haled into court, charged with brand changing, but he was not convicted. It is said that after his release Barbecue Campbell paid him five thousand dollars cash to show him how the brand was changed, and to stop stealing XIT cattle.

The rustler had registered the Star Cross brand, and this is how he rewrote it from the XIT:

Note that the stem of the T would often slant a little in the burning, due to the brander's carelessness or to the natural contours of a cow's hide. That slant was ideal for making two strokes of the five-pointed star.

Too many tributes and too many books, a lot of them the veriest drivel, have already been written about the most famous cowboy of all time. Americans tend to over-sentimentalize a man they love, endowing him with quite unnecessary halos. Rest assured that Will Rogers would not have appreciated most of the gushing heard about him immediately after his death. "I never met a man I didn't like," Will is quoted, for instance, and of this casual statement some orators and writers made much. If Will actually said that—which is doubtful—he said it in a moment of careless small talk. Will was no saint. He never traveled with any saints, or did any business with them. He met plenty of extremely rough men and women during his lifetime, and while he might never have aggressively hated any one (for hate is a stupid, cancerous thing), he surely never liked a lot of them. He wasn't always famous. He began life humbly, a poor cowwaddy with no future and with few assets save an abiding sense of humor. He developed his roping skill and his wise-cracks into a definite artistry and became a showman, and he took advantage of the motion picture and its highly skilled press agentry without getting the big head, all of which we can respect and admire him for. Best thing we can say about him

now, however, is that he was thoroughly human, as simple and
homely as his old dogiron brand:

We do not know why Will chose the dogiron, or andiron,
for his brand. It seems likely that he just designed something,
then named it for what it resembled.

Will entered the cow business in 1890 with eighty dogies.
The obscure, part-Indian cowboy doubtless felt a normal pride
in burning them as his own. They multiplied and became valuable, so that when wanderlust struck young Will one day he
could sell them for enough money to go—contrary to his parents' wishes—to far away Argentina to punch cows. He didn't
stay there long, because he went to South Africa to have such
fun as he could in the Boer War. The fun turned out to be
grime and blood and death, as any other soldier's fun always
does, but Will luckily got back home.

Clem Rogers, Will's father, had embraced more than two
hundred sections, but by the year 1900 activity on the ranch
languished. Will came back from his travels, saw little future
in the cattle business, and so got a job with his lariat rope on
the vaudeville stage. Most of the world is familiar with his rise
after that. Most of the world, too, especially most of the cowboys, are justly proud of and for him.

Will's father used the CV brand on cattle and J4 on horses.
Will had been born in the old double log house on the ranch,
and there he constantly saw the fireplace and andirons. Maybe
this association accounts for his selection of his own brand. He
referred to all three brands often in his speeches and his writings.

Herb McSpadden became manager of the Rogers ranch in
recent years. He found an old andiron branding iron, knew it

had been Will's, and so put it back into use just to keep Will's brand going. Herb was repairing an orchard fence and found a rusted J4 iron, too, holding down some hog wire. That was before Will's death, and Herb cleaned off the iron, branded a few ponies and sent the iron to Will in Beverly Hills, California.

Now that Will is gone, efforts are being made to keep the line of andiron, CV and J4 brands going onto Oklahoma stock for endless generations. Will would appreciate that a whole lot more than he would a "Rogers Monument" on top of some high mountain.

It is an old American custom to ask who or what was "first". We don't worship our ancestors but we do like to know which ones were illustrious, and if they weren't illustrious we like to know that they got there ahead of anybody else. A common question, since Texas is generally known as the first and biggest of the cattle states, is "Who was the first Texas cattle baron?"

In meticulous fact, Arizona, not Texas, cradled the cattle industry in this nation, for Spaniards first brought cows into what is now the United States [1] at a point near the present-day Douglas, Arizona. Sentiment and tradition, however, often over-weigh the minutiae of history, so that to all effects and purposes Texas is "first" both in cattle statistics and background. Similarly, some Spanish hopeful, probably Nicolás Saez, would have to be listed as the first man to brand cattle in Texas, although it seems likely that Stephen F. Austin was the "first" Anglo-Saxon cattleman there. He is illustrious enough

[1] The reader will remember, of course, that all our American cattle are of foreign ancestry, having been introduced to this continent by Spanish explorers and settlers. Nearest we had to the cow was the bison. Similarly all horses, asses, and mules were introduced by Spaniards.

for several other reasons to be worthy of this additional honor.

Texas was still in the political cradle when Austin began using his brand. It was known as the "old Spanish brand", suggesting that Austin did not design it but adopted it from some prior use. It was among the first recorded in Brazoria, oldest county in the Lone Star State.

Stephen F. Austin had a destiny far beyond his efforts as a cow puncher. In 1833, before his trip to Mexico where he was imprisoned, this Father of Texas sent two hundred cows to his sister by his faithful slave, Simon. Beyond that we know little of his work as a cattleman. This gift probably ended his ranching endeavors, because he died shortly after his return from Mexico.

Nevertheless the brand persisted through use by his heirs and relatives, the Austins and Perrys. Stephen S. Perry, Jr., great-grandnephew of the famous colonizer, in recent years has been perpetuating the family and state legend by carrying the brand into its second century. Garrison Hall, beautiful new building on the campus of Texas University at Austin (the state capital, named for Stephen F.), is adorned appropriately with thirty-two brands carefully selected from thousands of those best known in Texas. First to be placed there was this "old Spanish brand" of Steve Austin's cows:

If a tendency is noted in this book and in all other discussions of branding and cattle raising to refer often to Texas and the southwestern border in general, that is only natural and normal. Many fine beeves of course originate on the ranges of Oregon and Wyoming and the Dakotas and even in the Canadian provinces, but the American cattle business has been and is yet essentially *South*western; both cattle and horses came first into the United States through Mexico; in the Southwest grass and browse and climate, especially climate, make more lands fitted peculiarly for cattle raising.

Somewhat away from the Rio Grande or the Gadsden Purchase, however, is the stamping ground of a memorable stockman who knew nothing of Texas, who despised Mexicans and their languid *mañana* philosophy of living, and who contributed a great deal to the development of the range cattle industry. Like Stephen F. Austin he was a pioneer, but there the similarity stops; whereas Austin was a bachelor, this other brave man had nineteen wives. His name was Brigham F. Young.

Any man who herded nineteen wives will of course deserve and get immortality for that before any mention is made of his cattle, even if he had owned nineteen million of the latter. And it is true that Brigham Young lives in print and in memories only as the notorious or great (depending entirely on your point of view) Mormon pioneer. He headed the Mormon contingent which entered the vast Salt Lake Valley in 1847, made it a religious and agricultural oasis, founded Salt Lake City, began sending missionaries to all parts of the world. The cult multiplied, outsiders came in, demands for beef grew, and possibilities for raising cattle for shipment to other markets became apparent. Ideal grazing lands were located in parts of southern Utah and along the north rim of the Grand Canyon in Arizona.

When Indians killed Dr. James Whitmore in 1866, Brigham Young purchased his ranch holdings in the name of the Mormon church. John W. Young, one of Brigham's fifty-seven children, was sent to manage the new outfit. John made a successful manager, built the herd up to a maximum of ten thousand cattle and two thousand horses, earned thereby the commendation of his father and boss.

It seems a little bit shameful that so imaginative a man as Brigham Young did not find time to create his cattle brand. His brand *might* have been a conspicuous piece of range heraldry but, conceivably, he had constant naggings and troubles that distracted his mind. He left the brand selection to the lesser man, his son, and John made the brand simply a J W Y. It did become known as the "Church Brand", but when drouth wrecked the Mormons' stock raising enterprise the J W Y herd dwindled and disappeared. A protected bison herd grazes near John W. Young's ranch headquarters in highly colorful House Rock Valley today.[1]

Back in 1886 some of the better ranges in Texas, where cattle raising had mushroomed, had become over-grazed. The stock had to be moved to virgin territory or be allowed to perish. Much of it was shifted in small herds all the way westward to the Pacific Ocean, but one particular shipment, forwarded by the Continental Cattle Company, was destined to find a new home in the area south of Flagstaff and Holbrook, Arizona, towns now on the well worn transcontinental Highway 66. The new organization there was officially named the Aztec Cattle Company, but in just a few months it had acquired and deserved the designation of "Hashknife outfit".

A hashknife is a common kitchen tool. It has a round handle

---

[1] Brigham Young did have a personal brand—BY—which was stamped in the handles of all his implements and tools, and on the horns of some of his oxen, but not on his range stock. Although JWY was the "Church Brand" in Arizona, the Mormon church herds around Salt Lake were branded with the Christian cross †, changed later to ⚔ .

on top for gripping, a stout shank leading to a curved knife. With this knifeblade meat, vegetables and fruit can be rendered into hash in a bowl. It is a peculiar weapon but on occasions it has been used very effectively, too, on human flesh. It might rightly be regarded as symbolic of fierceness and destruction. Certainly "Hashknife outfit" became an appropriate nickname for the Aztec Cattle Company personnel.

The late Will C. Barnes, an authority on cattle history and one who witnessed the development of the livestock industry in Arizona and New Mexico, was running cattle in that section when the Hashknife entered and virtually crowded the small outfits out. In describing the Hashknife, Mr. Barnes states, "those Texas cows could stand more grief, use less food, drink less water, and bear more calves than any cows that ever wore a brand. The owners also brought with them a bunch of men of equal meanness, wildness, and ability to survive most any-thing in the way of hardships and sheriffs." Hashknife riders managed to take part in all projects of a lawless or exciting type. Traveling to the Tonto Basin, they participated in the Graham-Tewksbury feud and the Pleasant Valley sheep and cattle war.

For several years the Hashknife flourished. Private records show that they branded sixteen thousand calves during the sea-son of 1888. Growth of vegetation over their range of thirty-six hundred square miles was not rapid enough to feed the ever increasing herds. Years of drought accompanied by hard win-ters played havoc with their cattle. In 1900 the stock which re-mained was shipped out. The brand changed hands several times and at present is owned by the Babbitt Brothers at Flag-staff who use it on a few cows near Winslow.

Cattle of a dozen different outfits now graze over the two-million-acre pasture, once the home of thousands of Texas critters all wearing the brand resembling this much used kitchen tool: ⊥

The whole world knows that gold glittered once in California and caused a westward stampede. Men, women and children from every social stratum back East rushed to the Pacific coast, venturing everything, even their very lives, to get some of the easy wealth. Among them traveled Henry Miller, whose ancestors probably spelled it Mueller, because he was a German butcher's son. Henry himself had come from the old country shortly before.

Henry, however, found himself bewildered at the Yankees' madness in taking the actual yellow metal from the streams and hills. Gold to him was like money, simply a medium of exchange. One could not eat it, nor wear it for clothing, nor dwell on it, nor use it for shelter. Better that an immigrant boy should make his wealth in more usable form. Better his "gold" should be something that he could understand. He understood meats because he had worked in his father's butcher shop. Accordingly, in this new and flamboyant California, Henry Miller set up a butcher shop of his own.

The Yankee shrewdness and genius for expansion is always contagious to smart minds, however, and Henry quickly perceived that if he were going to run a butcher shop he might as well create his own source of meat supply. He observed that all the factors conducive to successful beef production existed in the valleys and mountains around him, so he began raising his own beef. Pretty soon the process became so interesting and profitable that he could not afford to spend his time bloodying his hands with cleaver and knife, ribs and rumps and loins and guts. He sold his butcher shop and became a rancher, full fledged. Prosperity was so widespread then that he spent most of his time for a while just buying land and cattle.

In time Henry Miller's holdings became so vast and his herds so large that he probably never knew the full extent of either. After land and cattle—a desired source of supply—he went back into the handling of them for market. Miller beeves came to be slaughtered in Miller packing houses. Miller fields soon were irrigated by water from Miller irrigation canals. Ultimately Miller enterprises were financed by loans from Miller banks. Henry's reclamation, power, financial, real estate, packing, agricultural, and livestock projects he operated as one great unit. No other cattleman in California has ever approached him in financial achievement.

After several successful years Miller formed a partnership with Charles Lux, but Miller always managed the outfit. The partnership prospered and in time the Miller-Lux range extended from southern Oregon, through Nevada, to a point below Bakersfield, California. This was not one continuous strip, but the holdings were so situated that herds from Oregon could be driven to California and always bed down for the night on Miller-Lux land.

In the course of so much buying, changing, enlarging, and moving of herds, not one but several brands came under the Miller and then the Miller-Lux ownership. Part of the cowboys' task was that of crossing out a former owner's brand and burning on a new one. This was accomplished in that era in either of two ways. The new owner might simply burn a straight line through the old brand, just as an editor might draw a single straight line through a word in a manuscript, and put the new brand directly under the old one. Or, instead of the line through the discarded brand, the discarded one might be repeated under itself to show that it was inoperative, and the new one burned alongside. The latter process, more tedious, was thought to indicate a distinction between cows that had legally changed hands and cows that had been stolen, but the obvious inconvenience of this repetition method made it unpopular. Some of the Miller-Lux cattle would have looked like billboards in time, with so many changes of hands, if the repetition method had been strictly adhered to; and so, for that matter, would the stock of other ranchers throughout the West.

Miller and Miller-Lux outfits had two favorite brands. They were double H, and S Wrench:

They were burned on the hip and neck respectively. Both supposedly were created by Henry Miller, but what significance either design had in his mind seems now to be unknown.

As with every other superlatively big something achieved by man in California or anywhere else, the glory of the Miller-Lux cattle kingdom has faded. Miller-Lux lands and legends still abound, but the remnants of once populous herds have been absorbed by younger outfits, and with them the Double H and the S Wrench have become just two more historic cattle brands.

As already indicated, the reason why the American cattle industry centers in the *South*west is partly historical, mainly climatic. Snow can fall and sleet can sting along the Mexican border, but likely as not tomorrow and all next week will be days of sunshine so brilliant and dependable that the cowpunchers can work in shirt sleeves. This fact is now making the border states dominant in the herding of those relatively new animals known as dudes (to be discussed in detail later) and it has also had a profound influence on the cattlemen's incomes. Cattle are simply pounds of edible, salable beef, on foot. Every pound used up in combating blizzards is three cents or ten cents, or whatever, out of the rancher's pocket at market time.

This salient fact has swept many a northern cattle rancher right into bankruptcy, killed off many a courageous man who, battling nothing worse than a Texas drought, might have made a go of it. Windmills are pretty good weapons with which to whip a long dry spell, but you still can't do a thing about temperatures that drop under zero and hibernate there. Conrad Kohrs of Montana, for instance, counted eighteen thousand two hundred frozen cattle bearing the proud CK brand, from his herd of twenty-one thousand that started the hard winter of 1886–87. Over a thirty-year period his losses of CK cattle amounted to fifty-two thousand head. This from one cattleman alone, not from all the hundreds of others who have braved the blizzards of Montana, Wyoming, the Dakotas, and other high cold states. Contrast Conrad Kohrs with present-day cattlemen who have been paid for killing emaciated cattle by a beneficent government. Nobody sent Kohrs a letter of sympathy, much less a remunerative check.

Despite all that, Kohrs was outstanding among Montana's early leaders. He entered the cattle business in Deer Lodge Valley in 1862. His business enjoyed a steady growth in spite of the weather, which is tribute enough to his perseverance and strength, so that the CK outfit became probably the largest in the Northwest. Ninety thousand head at one time fattened on the grasses of Kohrs' estate, and thirty trainloads of CK cattle went to Rosenbaum Brothers in Chicago at one fall shipping. It was said that more CK cattle came to the historic Union Stock Yards than any other brand before or since.

The CK property has shrunk in size, and although the CK brand is still in use, the personal career of Conrad Kohrs of course is over. But his record stands in the Northwest as a constant inspiration to younger men who must defy hardships, dangers, bankers, and cold.

Franciscan padres were building missions, spreading the gospel, and branding cattle in the American Southwest a century before Paul Revere made his ride. Each mission had its herds and branding irons. Dating back to that era of conquest and exploration are two picturesque California ranches.

Between Los Angeles and San Diego the present-day traveler unknowingly passes through one of them, a beautiful property called Rancho Santa Margarita, running this brand:

$$\overline{\eth}$$

Situated on lands which at one time belonged to the San Luis Rey Mission, this ranch has played an important part in the romantic history of the Golden Bear state. Generations ago, at a carefully chosen spot on the Santa Margarita, Indians under the supervision of the padres built a large adobe house with thick walls and heavy tiled roof. Fine architects they were, for that structure still houses the offices of the ranch and is the residence of its manager. Hills which roll toward the sea, tall silent palms, the blue waters of the Pacific, long white bunkhouses, cattle and blooded saddle animals wearing the ranch brand are loved by those who live there. Still visible is a faint trail which winds through the pastures, a trail once made dusty by the feet of barefoot Indians as they followed the fathers to the next mission; it is the original El Camino Real.

Like the Santa Margarita, El Tejon [1] ranch near Bakersfield

---

[1] Pronounced *el tay-HONE.* Translation: The Badger.

dates back to the days of the dons and links the old California with the new. Its brand suggests a cross on a mission arch or dome, and is burned thus:

This ranch is rich with legends of bandits, Indians and treasure. It is very old yet is a modern producer of beef. Fences enclose its three-hundred-thousand-acre pasture, and it is a twelve-mile drive from the front gate to the porch of the headquarters structure. Adult Mexican cowboys tell thrilling stories about El Tejon, stories told to them by their grandparents, who were born right there. The complexion of these representative Spanish ranchos is but little changed; the settings and characters are essentially the same as when romantic drama was being lived there in the Sierra Nevada foothills generations ago.

Picturesque? Ha! America has produced but five picturesque men: the Indian, the trapper, the prospector, the cowboy, and the Mexican. On ranches of the old Southwest are still to be seen individuals who combine the show merits of two of them, the cowboy and the Mexican; at any roundup or fiesta the other three are likely to wander in. They are a link with our most florid yesterday. If ranches such as the Santa Margarita and El Tejon can be kept intact forever, Californians will render a distinguished service indeed to their fellow Americans.

2.

Now in the matter of achieving that desirable but elusive state which we call fame, a great many American ranch owners have been forced to play second fiddle, or even third, fourth, and fifth fiddle, to the grand barons who struck it rich through luck or genius or circumstance. Nevertheless, not all of these lesser range folk have been content to stay unknown. They have catered to their vanities, and had a modicum of fun, by simply buying at least a local fame of their own through their local newspapers.

Beginning about 1886 when open-range cattle raising was at its peak, the publication of cattle brands in western newspapers came into general practice, and in a few instances has persisted to this day. Sometimes page after page of the weekly papers catering to range folk would carry little ads of one, two, three, or maybe six inches by one column, picturing individual ranch brands and ear-marks and usually giving a verbal description of these also. The ads were inexpensive; twenty cents per column-inch, or perhaps up to fifty cents. For less than ten dollars a month a rancher might have a standing ad proclaiming his brand and the location of his spread to the world, or at least to such of the world as read that paper. Incidentally, that was an era when papers were read with A to Z thoroughness; books and radios and sophisticated magazines hadn't thrust themselves too much into the scene.

Those ranch advertisements served no practical purpose whatsoever except that a few were used as a warning to rustlers. They were not directed at the probable customers of the rancher, the packing houses or buyers to whom he might sell his marketable steers. They were published only for the sight of his competitors, families who were likely to be friends and neighbors as well, and for the few village or townsfolk in the community where he traded and where the paper was printed. In the knowledge that these people did see his brand each week, a ranch owner had full recompense for the money he paid out. Somehow he associated publication with importance. His naïveté in this must not be regarded with amusement or contempt, because America today is still full of city sophisticates who will sell their souls to have their names in the papers. Ask any city editor!

Those early ranch ads of course were extremely crude and quaint, but no more so than any other small advertisements of

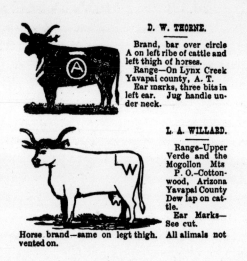

D. W. THORNE.

Brand, bar over circle A on left ribe of cattle and left thigh of horses.
Range—On Lynx Creek Yavapai county, A. T.
Ear marks, three bits in left ear.   Jug handle under neck.

L. A. WILLARD.

Range—Upper Verde and the Mogollon Mts
P. O.—Cottonwood, Arizona Yavapai County Dew lap on cattle.
Ear Marks—
See cut.

Horse brand—same on legt thigh.   All alimals not vented on.

their era. Practically all of them pictured the brand not alone but actually on a steer. The "art" work was the poorest sort of woodcut at first, a hand-tooled silhouette of a steer with the brand cut on the side in exaggerated size. Later when more pride came into the advertising business, and editors began to cooperate with their ranch customers a little more, the cuts became crude line drawings with some detail included, and brands were reduced more nearly to proper proportion. On this page, for instance, are pictures of the *Bar Over Circle A* of D. W. Thorne, and the *L W Connected* of L. A. Willard. Note

carefully, too, the wording, the type faces, and even the typo-
graphical errors, all exactly as they originally appeared in newspapers in Arizona Territory.

In the above illustrations you will note a rank discrepancy,
or at least the trained western eye will note one. The animal
pictured by Mr. Willard is not the conventional steer, but is a

$1,000 REWARD.

☞ I desire to call attention to my
marks and brands for cattle, as shown in
cut. I sell no stock cattle, and will pay
$1,000 reward for the arrest and convic-
tion of any person or persons unlawfully
handling cattle in the following brand
and marks;

J. H. HAMPSON.

P. O.—EL PASO, TEXAS.   Ranch P. O.
—CLIFTON, ARIZONA.

cow in the literal sense. Sometimes bulls would be pictured, but
female bovines with udders were—for some reason not at all
clear—taboo. The story is that Mr. Willard simply wanted to
be contrary. He walked into the editor's office, ordered and
paid for his ad, and bucked when the editor sketched off a steer.

"Make mine a cow, or don't run it at all!" Mr. Willard ordered, and so it was done. One old-timer says that this cut, and one run by Shipp Brothers showing a cow jumping over the moon, pictured the only females he ever saw in these ranch advertisements. Perusal of the old newspaper files tends to bear him out.

Even so, the two above are relatively conventional and uninteresting. It was inevitable that some rancher with a sense of humor would see possibilities in his advertisement. We do not know who was first to shock the editor and the public by making his steer a caricature, but J. H. Hampson was among the early ones. Hampson's *Double Circle* has been a well known iron since 1883.

Mr. Hampson came out boldly with a warning, at the start of his ad, and sort of dared anybody to touch his brand. And then, according to the result credited to the Mills Engraving Company, he waxed funny. On page 151 is the illustration and general layout for his otherwise emphatically businesslike announcement.

The above brand is high up on left hip instead of low down, as it appears in the cut.

T. B. CARTTER,

Postoffice Address—WALNUT GROVE, Arizona. Brand and Ear Marks same as is represented in the bove cut.

Range.—Walnut Grove and vicinity, Yavapai county. Arizona

That still doesn't reach the ultimate, but it probably was reached by Mr. Tom Cartter over at Walnut Grove. Tom avowed that his ranch was the rockiest in North America. He chuckled about it often, and swore that he had to put boots on every one of his steers to keep them from getting sore feet. So when he started running his ranch advertisement he pictured his branded steer as on page 152.

Now don't ask why Tom went a step farther and had the face of Satan engraved in place of the steer's head. It may have been a momentary whim of the editor, but most likely it further reflected the mood of the rancher himself. A steer darn sure can be satanic at times, as Tom would have known.

E. H. WITHERELL,

Postoffice Address—PRESCPTT, ARIZONA.
Cattle and horses branded as shown in cuts· below

Ear Marks—Underbit in left and upperbit in right

Range—Lonesome Valley and Black Hills Yavaj ai Co., Arizona.
☞ Also owner of the following irons,

Left thigh.   Left shoulder.   Right thigh.   Lett Side

☞ A liberal reward will be paid for the return of any ᴄstrays to my ranch. I also wish it understood that no "monkeying" with my stock will be tolerated, and any person who seeks, off of my herd, to illegitimately increase his own, will have the hot soup of justice everlastingly pumped into him.

Ed Witherell's advertisement is a typical example of honest pride in brands, also of the Gothic or "studhorse" type favored then, and of the curt warnings to rustlers. Ed's edict under the pointing hand (which was held as a clever printer's trick in that day) meant exactly what it said. Below is Ed's contribution to ballyhoo.

3.

In discussing, on the preceding pages, historic and existing ranches of America we necessarily limited ourselves to a very few of those that have achieved enduring fame. Often theirs are mere thumbnail sketches, but even from that abridged list it has pained us to omit many other worthy subjects known and loved throughout the West. Still more, however, must we restrict ourselves in presenting representative foreign brands.

The cowboy as the world now knows him is a creature peculiarly North American, and yet some cowboy of course has been herding cows in China, Russia, Africa, South America, Australia and practically every other foreign land for a long, long time. In point of fact, *El Gaucho* of the Argentine is every whit as much a storybook character as the most dashing cowboy Texas or California ever produced; he has just lacked the press agentry. He may even achieve the latter in a few more years, because as this chapter rolls from an American typewriter, on the front porch of an Arizona ranch, this very day's newspaper headlines proclaim the fact that the American navy is being fed on Argentine beef. There seems to be some financial, and especially some political, justification for this odd fact, but the American ranches cannot understand such politics and such economy. The upshot may be a national study of conditions in the Argentine.

Ranches in Argentina are called *estancias*—"ace-TAHN-see-ahs". There as here they are just expanses of land more suitable for grazing than for anything else. It is said that grass grows with more luxury there than in North America, but this is doubtful. Inevitably the same general conditions in herding cows must hold, and so the same requisites in branding are found. Nor is cattle branding materially different in Argentina —or, for that matter, anywhere else in the world—from branding in the U. S. A. The same experiments have been tried in introducing new methods of branding, but in general cows are still trademarked by use of hot irons.

The actual brand may be more florid than the average is in practical-minded Texas, but this will be just a reflection again of the Latin love for pretty things, as we have already seen in the case of the Mexican and early Spanish brands. In fact the grand *estancias* of Argentina are comparable in most ways to the Chihuahuan rancho of Don Luis Terrazas, previously described. Aristocratic Argentinian stockmen are likely to be *magníficos* with more money than they know how to spend. They often go to Europe to drop some of it at the fashionable resorts. They live in veritable palaces, surrounded by formal gardens. They have house parties and *gaucho* contests of skill, just as our American rodeos are comparable to the jousts and tournaments of heraldry in mediaeval times. Of course there are many lesser ranches struggling humbly to make both financial ends meet. These latter in the long run must bear the burden of the industry as a whole, just as the little men in any industry anywhere are the important ones because of their numbers and their fortitude. Unfortunately, they are the least interesting.

Liebig's Extract of Meat Company, Limited, was one of

Argentina's largest. Liebig's have owned as many as half a
million cattle at once, and during one season burned their *Marca
Trébol* (clover leaf)

on one hundred and eighty thousand cattle in the Provincia de
Corrientes alone. The original vast Liebig *estancia* has been
broken down into several smaller ones in recent years. Estancia
Garruchos is a Liebig subsidiary widely known. Besides Argentina, Liebig's *estancias* are operated in Paraguay and Uru-
guay. The *Marca Trébol* is perhaps the best known brand in
all of South America.

A close rival is the Argentinian Estancia Huetel owned by
Señora Unzue de Casares, which is famous both as a social
center and as a producer of fine cattle. The ranch home is a
palatial estate where many of the important visitors to the
Argentine are entertained.

Next in importance as ranching goes, perhaps, are the ranches
of Australia. In that continent, ranches are called stations. Don't
ask why. It is all due to the peculiarity of the people, who speak
English rather than American. We Yankees can never understand why the English refer to "the mail" as "the post", either.
True, we ourselves refer to our mailman as "the postman",
but—! Stations perhaps is as good a name as any.

Victoria River Downs Station in northern Australia is probably the largest ranch in the world (but King Ranch in Texas
is the largest privately owned). Leased and operated by a corporation, it embraces approximately seven and a half million acres,
a territory larger than our states of Rhode Island, Delaware and
Connecticut combined. Its top count in cattle, however, has
been only seventy-five thousand head or so.

Wave Hill Station, also in Northern Territory, had seven thousand and one square miles and a maximum of about fifty thousand cattle and fifteen hundred horses, mules and donkeys. However, it was distinguished by having several hundred riding and pack camels, too. This property was founded originally in 1870, and in 1914 was purchased by the Australian Investment Company, a private concern. The brand of its founders, an unromantic 62U, was then changed to the equally unromantic TVH.

In Queensland, the Strathmore Station boasts two million three hundred thousand acres, and Vanrook almost two million. Roundups, marketing, branding, leasing, droughts, all are a part of the routine there as in every other station, ranch, rancho, *estancia* or whatever, anywhere in the world.

Not exactly foreign, but still in a far distant land, is the ranching industry of Hawaii. It is not big enough to be of worldwide importance financially, and yet its history is worthy of mention. Following Captain Cook's discovery of the Islands, Captain Vancouver introduced the first cows in 1793. King Kamehameha issued a strict edict forbidding any killing of the animals, which had been planted at several places in Hawaii, and when the taboo was finally removed large herds had developed in the plains and mountains there. Most of the cattle had become wild.

In 1830 John P. Parker of Newton, Massachusetts, established the ranch which still bears his name. It extended from the Pacific to a point ninety-five hundred feet up on Mauna Kea, so that soil, rainfall and other climatic conditions vary widely on the big ranch. Parts of it can support one steer to every three acres, other parts one steer to every fifty acres. Sheep are grazed on the higher levels. Purebred strains have been encouraged for all its stock. Honolulu is the main market, and Parker sheep and steers, branded by native cowboys with the Lazy P brand, furnish most of the meat for the territory. Several other historic ranches operate in Hawaii, but the Lazy P with its half million acres is by far the largest, and is widely known in South Pacific lands.

CHAPTER X

COWROGRAPHY OFF THE COWS

By no means all of the escutcheons owned pridefully by the knights of western America have been burned onto their cows, horses, sheep, goats, burros, women, or pigs. In general, it is true, the rancher has used the brand on his animate possessions since he felt they were most likely to be stolen or most likely to stray. But because he invariably came to love his brand and feel a fierce and sentimental loyalty toward it, he has also placed it on practically everything else under his sun.

The beautiful new rock "bunkhouse" on the grounds of the Texas Cowboy Reunion Association at Stamford, Texas, has dozens of historic cattle brands carved like epitaphs in stones set around its walls. The building was designed as a meeting place for old-time cowpunchers, and to finance it the backers announced that any person who wanted his favorite brand carved there, or who wanted to honor some old rancher friend, could have a stone for fifteen dollars. Instantly the money began to roll in.

When Texas University, which was endowed by revenues from cattle grazing lands, built an imposing new mess hall recently (called, appropriately, the Chuckwagon), the main decorative theme was formed of a few cattle brands carefully selected from a list of thousands.

The coat of arms over the entrance to Pioneer Hall at the teachers college in Canyon, Texas, is a steer head encircled by historic Panhandle brands, and branding irons form the most popular exhibit held by the museum inside.

Sixty or seventy brands are worked into the doors of the elevators of the new Potter County courthouse at Amarillo, Texas, and McMurry College at Abilene emphasizes its collection of irons. The large and elaborately printed menu of the largest restaurant in Midland, Texas, is adorned not with pictures of tempting fruit, meats, or other viands, but by about two hundred regional cattle brands; and, like as not, the tarts or cookies or molded gelatine or piecrust or cake icing which you will eat there will be ornamented with brands too.

The high purplish peak of Mount Franklin which dominates the skyline around the picturesque city of El Paso is desecrated by a gargantuan brand in the form of a white letter M, put there by enthusiastic and energetic undergraduates at the Texas College of Mines. "A Mountain" near the University of Arizona is branded from the same fire of sentiment, as are dozens of other hillsides, water tanks, roofs, campaniles, smoke stacks and such boasted by western schools. Indeed, the practice of giving the school athletes their "letters" is just another form of branding.

All such public manifestations of the branding urge, however, are to be expected. They might indicate that a bit of scholarly research has been done by the architects or builders or students or professors or others in charge, but do they adequately reflect the sentiments of the individual cowman? Where does the individual ranch family use its brand, aside from on its livestock, chuck wagons, saddles, harness, and tools?

A typical ranch which has endured drouth and disease and financial panics long enough to have traditions is likely to be branded from the highway on. First thing you will see may be the rural mail box, bearing not the name John Smith but Smith's ranch brand, the J Bar. More than likely the proprietor there is called not John but Jaybar Smith, just as Bar B Q Campbell was never known by anything but Barbecue Campbell, and John Chisum was always called Jinglebob Chisum. Two or three other mail boxes, put close together so the postman need make only one stop there, may bear as many more ranch brands. The postman and everybody else in the county will know whose boxes they are. For a rancher to have lettered his full name on his box might be construed as conceit, and would be unnecessary anyway. But it is never conceit to display one's cattle brand.

A sign or two along the turnoff road will bear more ranch brands plus guiding arrows. When you come to the front gate, the big post and perhaps the sliding latch will have a ranch brand burned somewhere on it. A few miles further, when you come in sight of the home windmill tower, you will see a brand on the windmill vane and maybe on the water tank too; the rancher's sons see to it that the brand is kept there.

Inside the home you will not be conscious of brands being intrusive, or overly used, but as you stay there you will discover more and more of them. Perhaps your first glance reveals a fireplace mantel which is an oak timber eight feet long, twelve inches wide and six inches thick. The six-inch side, facing out, will have the ranch brand burned into it at several places to make a very distinctive frieze. If some of the burns are rather crude, it will mean that one of the family sketched them there on some winter evening, using the poker as a running iron. (A common branding iron, incidentally, is about the best poker you can find, even for city use.) Beyond that, you are likely to find the brand almost anywhere. It may be appliquéed or

embroidered onto the bedspread and pillow slips—for wouldn't
this be more appropriate and satisfying than sewing on conventional French curves entwined around waterlilies, or some
other pattern created in a mail order factory? The table spread,
the leather chair bottom, the hooked rug, the children's school
books (the kids will ride branded horses or a branded car several miles to school) and the window curtains will all show
the brand. Branding irons themselves make excellent ornamental curtain rods. The longer you stay, and the more such
ranch homes you visit, the more places you will discover where
brands are applied.

Back in 1919 a young rancher in South Dakota, named Roy
Pascal, went to Chicago with a shipment of cows, managed to
crash elite society there, and came home with a city girl bride.
Spunkily, the bride adjusted herself to the ranch environment
in no time at all, although her family felt that she was just a self-
sacrificing missionary to the heathen, or words to that effect.
They kept sending her "encouraging" letters, which she
ignored because she was busy learning to cook and shoot and
ride. After a while, when they learned she was to have a baby,
they sent out a special nurse for her, but she promptly shipped
the nurse back and had her baby in easy, civilized western style.
The family still wasn't daunted, however. Grandmother sent a
great box of toys, enough to entertain the youngster until he
should reach the age of ten or twelve years. Among the toys
was a set of expensive blocks. They were square blocks, hand
painted, lacquered, decorated not only with the A B C alphabet
but with exquisite pictures of flowers, bluebirds, and ribbon
designs.

The young father saw the blocks and snorted. "Gimme them
damned things!" he commanded.

He threw the whole set into the fireplace fire, went outside
and whistled to one of his ranch hands. They conferred for
a moment and before sundown the baby boy (still a suckling
infant, mind you) possessed a set of blocks entirely appropriate
to his heritage and probable rearing. They held no bluebirds,
no flowers, no ribbons, not even any paint. They didn't even
include any A B C's. They were just cubes of pine with designs
burned on them like this:

The typical western mother in a ranch home is more nearly
a Mother than anywhere else in the world. Her energy and
tenderness are indispensable, and—what is more—appreciated.
In the old days the ranch wife and mother might not see another
woman for three to six months at a time; nowadays, however,
she is likely to buck a little and demand to go over to the neighbors' for a visit (seven miles) or even in to town every two or
three weeks. Meanwhile she is too thoroughly busy to develop
any form of self-pity. She has a million and one duties, but she
manages to find time for her flower garden as well. Almost
surely she will maneuver to get the ranch brand into her
flowers.

She—or you—can plant any of several dainty ground-
clinging varieties and in a few weeks have a brand design growing and blossoming beautifully. Mrs. Cleota Webb on the
"Spider Web" ranch (called that by the cowboys) planted a
lot of dwarf white flowers on a slope below the ranch windmill,
so that she could irrigate it in dry spells. She stuck up a few
pieces of stovewood and ran a rag string around them to keep
careless men off. In about two months, bless Pat if her flowers

hadn't created a white design about fifty feet across that looked like this:

Old man Webb was more proud of it than his wife was. He told his three sons and his daughters to help their mother care for it, and he told his cowboys that he'd personally cut their guts out if one of them ever harmed that big flower brand. It was visible for more than five miles, but he drove in to town and brought business friends out, plying them with barbecue roasted in a pit and served under a tree where they could see the flowers at close range. On their thirty-fifth wedding anniversary, that same spring, he went in to town and had the jeweler make mother a brooch of gold set with little diamonds, and when he paid his two thousand dollars for it, it looked just like the bed of flowers in miniature.

But one week later that spring he purchased a herd of yearlings, and was driving them toward his branding corrals. He and his men pushed them slowly up the long lane, past the bunkhouse and blacksmith shop, and were moving them right by the ranch residence itself when Mrs. Webb came busily onto the front porch to shake crumbs out of a table cover. A bull snorted. The strange noise and motion had alarmed him. Fear gleamed instantly in all the animals' eyes and of one accord they stampeded. Two minutes later the beautiful flower brand was a mass of unrecognizable hoofprints in dirt and mud.

Mrs. Webb's flower-bed brand is the most elaborate one the present authors have ever seen, but some remarkable effects have been made by trimming hedges into brand designs.

Flowering hedges were noted in which the white or red brand shone against a background of green. Naturally, this was in California, where everything seems to vie with everything else in producing profuse blooms. Privet, some of the thicker conifers, and innumerable vines have been trained into brand designs by patient and painstaking ranch women and girls, who invariably won thereby the hearty approbation of all visitors as well as of their own menfolks.

In New Mexico there is a ranch where—believe it or not!— even the apple trees grow apples having the ranch brand. Great big juicy red apples so fragrant they'd make a mummy hungry, each bearing a neat Bar V P brand like this:

Of course Nature has a little help in this from the ranch children. They stick on bits of tape just as the apples start rapid coloring, and the sun does the rest. Then they remove the tape, polish the apple, wrap it in cellophane.

The relatively few people who were so fortunate last fall as to get one or more of these super-extra-de-luxe apples were delighted to pay ten cents each for them, which is why the Bar V P children soon had plenty of Christmas money in hand. The trouble must have been considerable, the wastage great, and all that; but our point is that the ranch brand was used instead of a Mickey Mouse cartoon.

All manner of jewelry has been made in brand design. Exquisite, blue-green turquoise, cut and polished by Navajo Indians, will add color to a silver bracelet in which is cut the Quarter Circle W or the Flying X or the Seven Slash Eight or the Forked Lightning. Rings and watch chains and stick pins and "costume" jewelry in the cow country are likely to carry coats of arms from the range, and the twenty-seven-jeweled Elgin which Sonny gets for graduation probably will have papa's beloved ♥ design engraved prominently on the case. Barring that, it may have his own new ranch brand, papa having given him an additional present of fifty yearlings with which to launch a cattle career of his own.

Spurs very often have ranch brands engraved on them or otherwise put on them—and don't you ever think spurs aren't "jewelry", either. An otherwise uncouth and untidy range ranny may be wearing branded spurs that cost him a month's pay; they have hock shop value and they nourish his soul. Many a ranch son gets fancy spurs at Christmas or graduation time, instead of an Elgin.

Daughter may have branded jewelry and branded purses too. Purses made of the finest leather frequently are tooled to order with specific ranch brands. Expert craftsmen in old established houses like Porter's and Goldwater's at Phoenix make brand purses of such beauty as to lift the work definitely into the classification of art. Often the leather is calf hide with the hair left on and the brands carefully burned, just as they would be burned on living animals. Slunk hides, being especially silken, are favored for this.

Not all, but most, of the country's larger ranches have their private stationery for both business and personal use. This usually is not engraved because engraving would be "putting on the dog" and ranch folks despise pretense above everything else. On the other hand, printed stationery has definite business value and can be bought in quantities as cheap as or cheaper than little dabs of the unprinted kind. What to print on it? The answer is obvious! For convenience of distant folk, the postoffice and state will be listed too, but the rancher's name may not be. Probably the piece will look just about like this:

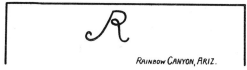

Rainbow Canyon, Ariz.

The busy girl mail clerk in Sears, Roebuck and Company at Chicago may not know that the brand reads Crazy R Ranch, but she *is* experienced enough to know that the postmaster in Rainbow Canyon, Arizona, will deliver catalogues and packages carrying no more address than the letterhead shows. She will even accept the rancher's bank check if it comes in signed or sealed only with the same cryptic design, because some ranchers—like old Winfield Scott years ago—either can't write at all or can't write legibly or just naturally prefer to sign with their brands. Courteous western banks grant them this privilege, knowing that such a man is likely to be more honest than the wealthiest city depositor, and knowing too that his inked or penciled brand, drawn by his own hand, is about as hard to forge as his signature would be. And a whole lot easier to read!

Burk Burnett's vast estate in Texas, reputedly launched in a lucky poker game with a hand of four sixes, uses stationery bearing the 6666 brand. In this case the brand is not just printed on the paper, but is on the side of a pictured steer just as if it were actually burned there. Rancho Santa Margarita in California has its brand (see p. 147) at the top of its stationery. The Bell Ranch of New Mexico has paper carrying its registered brand:

The stationery of Oliver Loving's ranch in Texas has to announce, in addition to showing its brand, that the ranch is located in *two* counties, Jack and Young, in what is known as

Lost Valley. Stationery used by H. Moffat Company shows the brand and a herd of steers. Seventy Six Ranch pictures not the steers but the range on which they graze—a lovely landscape of mountains and canyons and trees on each sheet of paper. Some corporations owning cattle enterprises have to list the corporation name and all their several addresses, and these corporations are almost always so impersonal as to omit the ranch brands. Which may be one reason why the firms are definitely disliked by the traditional, independent, self-reliant cattleman.

On the streets of Denver, Albuquerque, Fort Worth, Tucson, Billings, Calgary, Helena, and a hundred other cow towns, you can note branded automobiles and trucks parked on the street any day. They will be in front of the banks, the grocery stores, or perhaps the saddlery shops. The brands are usually just painted on the doors—put there expensively in gold by expert sign painters, for it would never do to have this an amateurish job. Once in a while a rancher will have a piece of rawhide, the hair still on, laced to his car and the ranch brand will be burned onto this, but such excellent displays usually are quickly removed in town by thieving souvenir hunters. A few ranch cars have brands tooled into their hub caps, and you may frequently see a genuine stamping iron welded onto the hood in place of the conventional radiator ornament.

Some ranches, notably the Belden Ranch at Pitchfork, Wyoming (owned by Charles Belden, who is also a distinguished range photographer, riding always with cameras strapped to his saddle like branding irons), and the Bell Ranch in New Mexico, own airplanes which carry the ranch brand prominently on the wings.

Cowboys brand almost anything they can get a rope on. It is

not uncommon for a hunter to shoot a buck and find a cattle brand burned on the deer's hip, put there by some prankish cowboy who lassoed a fawn. Jabalinas (wild hogs), coyotes, jackrabbits, elk, even bear, are likely to turn up branded. Desert terrapins have wandered too close to cattle trails and had brands carved on their horny houses.

It is an old story, too, about the tough cowboy's filing a notch in his six-shooter handle for every man he kills. In point of fact, very few cowboys bother to "tote" guns at all, and those who do are likely to have brands, not notches, filed thereon. We have seen one beautiful pistol with more than a hundred cattle brands worked minutely into its stock and barrel. Branding of course is about the best way to mark ownership of a fellow's rifle and shotgun. There are even stories of bullets being branded in range wars, so the dead man's friends would know for sure which outfit killed him.

Any old whangtail cowboy, having little of delicate artistry in his makeup but wishing he had more, is likely to satisfy his esthetic urge by carving his brand in the slick bark of a growing sycamore, aspen, manzanita, palo verde, "red man" or other tree. We have seen many a prickly pear ear, both thorny and thornless, scarred where nature has smoothed over the brand cut there by some cowpoke who probably lassoed, branded, and castrated a bull near by, or who may have just dismounted there for half an hour to smoke a cigarette and rest his horse. Cutting on any living tree is a miserable habit, for it invites rot and infection which may destroy the whole tree in a short while; but if you simply must do it, then do carve on some regional ranch brand. It is far better than catering to your own conceit by whittling your initials, and is much more picturesque.

Best branded ranch in history perhaps was Miller Brothers'
outfit in Oklahoma. Every animal and every piece of equipment it owned was burned or otherwise marked

101

The Millers took their mail from postoffice box 101 in Ponca
City. To telephone the ranch, you asked the operator for
Number 101. A letter mailed in New York City once was addressed only "1 0 1", but was delivered to the ranch in four
days. Part of the ranch reputation was due to its Show. The
101 Wild West Show toured America for years, introducing
millions of city folk to the genuine Wild West in dramatic manner. Small boys who had never seen a ranch, and who have
never yet seen one, even though they now have small boys of
their own, learned to play cowboy when the Hundred And
One came to town with its bronc busters and Indians and all
their spectacular doings. It is a downright shame that the Hundred And One Show lacked the prosperity to survive.

Here and there about the United States are a few individuals
and a few institutions that are doing a valuable work of preserving the lore of brands and branding. The institutions
include obscure museums or other departments in western col-
leges; their exhibits are representative collections of stamping
irons, but these almost invariably are limited to one state or
smaller region. They also have branding libraries, pitifully
small because there has been little of importance published
about the heraldry of the range. (See Preface.) By far the
best work in this fascinating field has been done by individuals.
In Houston, Texas, is an old grayhaired rancher known as a
gentleman gambler who is justly proud of his collection of

irons. In Los Angeles there are at least two collectors of importance. Several others have thirty, forty, fifty, mayhap even a hundred different irons, and are fairly well versed in the legends behind them. In Phoenix Edward E. Hartzell works in a leather store and collects brands that come through on the skirting leather from the tanneries—the only collection of tanned brands we know about; sometimes a little detail is lost in the tanning, but the collection is interesting. One and all, these folk are sincere hobbyists, pleasant to know and honest to deal with, quietly enjoying themselves while preserving precious bits of Americana.

It would be ungracious for the present authors to claim unequivocally that the branding iron and branding library collection of John Hale is the best in the world today, although unbiased authorities have repeatedly assured us that it is indeed the most noteworthy of all. His story therefore is included as representative of the iron hobbyists, with whatever apologies are due.

Mr. Hale was born in the Methodist parsonage at Stacyville, Iowa—certainly not a cowboy environment! But like many another he drifted into the saddle country as he grew up, was graduated from Kansas State College, then took a master's degree from the University of Southern California. He married Genevieve MacDonald on September 1, 1928, at Oceanside, California, where headquarters of the Rancho Santa Margarita are located. His business career included nine years as principal of the large Mesa Union High School in Mesa, Arizona, before he became district manager for a life insurance company.

Now, exactly how does any hobbyist get started at his hobby? How did John Hale happen to collect branding irons instead of postage stamps or butterflies?

"When I was a student in U. S. C.," he says, "I saw a collection of horseshoes displayed in a downtown jewelry store. Somehow it fascinated me, although I do not regard horseshoes as particularly interesting or important. I vowed some day to launch a western hobby of my own.

"When I was school principal at Mesa soon after that, my Masonic lodge there decided to honor a pioneer named J. J. Fraser, who had been a Mason for fifty-nine years and a cattleman longer than that. The honor—and worry—of being the manager of that program fell to me, and when I conferred with old Jack Fraser I discovered that the one thing in life of which he was proudest was his J F brand. Incidentally, his possessions included considerably more than that iron; they included such important items as ranches, mines, stores, and banks. I got Jack to talking. He told me his life story, ignoring his financial ventures but thrilling to the triumphs of his ranch brand. When I questioned him he admitted that *any* brand in existence as long as his was sure to have behind it a romantic story, fraught with the making and losing of fortunes, spiced with rustling, murder, hate, love, heartbreak, and success. He fondled the rusty old J F iron and gestured with it as he talked to me. For a long time I just sat there enthralled.

"We used that iron for a centerpiece at the banquet table, and my tribute to Jack that night so touched him that he came to me after adjournment and gave me his scepter with his own hand. It was almost as if some prince or king had knighted me; I could hardly speak to thank the old gentleman. I would rather have received that gift of his branding iron than one of his ranches, mines, or banks. I went right home and wrote down its history in meticulous detail, and while the J F is by no means my most valuable iron today, I think it is the one I prize the most. It started me not only in the hobby of collecting, it opened in me an appreciation of the whole broad heraldry of the American range."

Jack Fraser at this writing is eighty-four years old and so no longer settles his arguments with sheep men from the saddle. Most of his "augering" now is with other old-timers who loaf with him in the sunshine around Everybody's Drug Store in Mesa. Sometimes they have to call in "The Professor", John Hale, to settle their arguments about this brand or that, and Hale never fails to come away from them with some new bit of range lore.

The J F iron was hung in Hale's home over the fireplace that night after the banquet, and next day he set about getting some other irons. Before night he had run down two more. Next day he collected another, and by the end of the week he had ten. If the Mesa school trustees can now look back and remember perhaps that high school affairs sort of slumped for a few weeks along there, it was doubtless because their principal was mildly deranged. It seems that any hobbyist is likely thus to suffer!

And so the Hale collection after ten years numbers into the hundreds. The irons have, in a measure, run off with their owner now. If you doubt it, ask not John but Mrs. Hale! A pretty and exceptionally dainty young woman, she had to adjust herself rapidly to living with rusty, sometimes dirty, and always bulky and heavy pieces of metal showing no daintiness at all. The novelty of the first six or eight wore off immediately. The mantel space became crowded. The home den walls soon were filled. John would not tolerate storing them in the attic.

Today the Hale house is probably the most interesting western home you could ever expect to enter. It is a big house rambling around aimlessly, and branding irons thrust them-selves upon you at every turn. Give John half a chance there and you will miss dinner because he will be lifting iron after iron and telling you its story in detail.

With rare ingenuity Mrs. Hale has used the irons to make the home a delightful place to see, and if John languishes at all she will pick up the thread of story and go on with it. For that matter, so will ten-year-old Toby, whose real name is Evelyn Hale. When little Toby at age five went to kindergarten for the first time, the teacher drew a large A on the board and said, "Now, children, this is an A." Whereupon Toby took the chalk and drew a series of designs, informed the class that this was flying A, this was running A, this was walking A, this was open A, and so on with her brand explanations! She still shares her parents' enthusiasm for things of the range.

Now it is not easy to go out and collect several hundred branding irons from all corners of the world. For one thing, each iron has an intrinsic value of about ten dollars—that is, duplicating them at blacksmith shops would cost about that on the average—but beyond that is their possible appraised value as tokens. Ranches, especially old ranches, may have several of their irons around, but will not want to part with them, and the irons of ranches that have passed off the scene entirely may still be in possession of the people who used them, and will be highly prized. The scholarly collector's problem is to separate a rancher from his iron.

To this end John Hale has stooped to practically everything short of murder. On at least two occasions, he admits, it was necessary for him to snitch (steal is such a harsh word!) an iron. He is not above bribery, subtle or otherwise. But mostly he just comes out and asks for the iron or—in recent years—sits back and lets his earned reputation bring the irons to him. He has at last reached that state, heavenly to any hobbyist, wherein people are proud and anxious to have their irons in his collection.

Hardest of all to get, in Hale's experience, were not the rarest or the most valuable irons. The very hardest was a Terrazas iron, bearing the familiar brand. (See p. 121.) Don Luis Terrazas was the world's greatest cattle king, and since his ranch has not been out of existence more than twenty years, scores of Terrazas irons are still in existence. But Terrazas lived in Mexico, and died in political exile. His once great popularity had more than waned; it had slipped onto the negative side. Why are you interested in Terrazas? What do you want one of his irons for? Are his heirs trying to start something, a revolution maybe? Who are you? Why? . . . Why? . . . Why? . . . "What you do weeth thees iron, hah?" That sort of thing.

Hale wrote many letters when his personal efforts failed. He explained patiently, in great detail. He wrote in English. He wrote in Spanish. He wrote to most of the many Terrazas heirs. They did not understand, or were not interested in the Americano's aims. Finally he wrote to the American Consul in Chihuahua City, and this gentleman kindly interceded for him. Forthwith came a Terrazas iron with as polite a note of presentation as anybody could possibly want.

Irons seem to be more protected in Argentina than anywhere else. Hale was anxious to add the *Marca Trébol* iron of the great Estancia Garruchos to his collection, but Argentina is too far for hobbyist travel and letters again availed nothing. He tried to get one through his Masonic and Rotary Club affiliations, and failed. Finally, he chanced to make inquiry on his current insurance business letterhead, and the manager of the ranch chanced to be a policy holder in that same insurance company. The *Marca Trébol* iron was shipped to Mesa, Arizona, forthwith.

Another typical instance is shown in this quotation from a letter which Hale received from Señor Antonio Araujo, resident manager of historic El Tejon Rancho near Bakersfield, California:

"I am sending you an El Tejon iron which I have been more or less keeping as a souvenir myself; however, I know of no better place for it to be taken care of than in your collection. This iron was used by my father, who was on this ranch before I was born. From the best information I can get and from my recollection, this iron was made in the blacksmith shop on the ranch in 1877, was used by my father and handed down to me about thirty years ago, in 1904, when I was little more than a kid, and was graduating from being merely a plain rider to handling an iron during the branding season. I used it for many years and could not estimate how many cattle have been branded by this iron. It certainly would run into many thousands.

"This ranch consists of approximately three hundred thousand acres and was originally founded by some of the old Spanish dons, but the various grants were more or less collected together. The ranch is still run almost the same way that it has been for the last seventy-five years. Under normal conditions the ranch has approximately fifteen thousand head of cattle."

Since Will Rogers was the world's best known and best loved cowboy, and since he owned very few irons, the Rogers dogiron now in Hale's collection is ranked close, in sentiment at least, to that of Jack Fraser. It may be that the Rogers iron is the most valuable of the lot in every other way, but it is difficult to determine these things. Rarity of the iron, oddity of design, the story behind it, all these points must be appraised. There is no appreciable selling of branding irons as there is of stamps, for instance, and so there is no way of getting monetary appraisal. John Hale has been offered into the thousands of dollars for his collection as a whole, and has had flattering offers for individual irons from persons who were suddenly enthusiastic, but he does not sell. When a new iron duplicates one in his collection he gives it to another collector, or to some beloved friend as a special souvenir. Other collectors similarly honor him, and friends from everywhere now send him the irons they find.

"I correspond regularly with several other branding iron collectors," Hale says. "Some of them pursue the hobby scientifically, while others just collect. Good collectors in any field attempt to 'pedigree' the articles they collect, establishing the history and background of each. Some speak intelligently and authoritatively on their collections; others just have a mass of objects about which they know nothing.

"The brand collectors I know are all students and have gone to much trouble and research in building up the history of the irons they possess. One especially I have found to be well informed, not a collector of branding irons, but a man who has made his hobby a study of the history of the technique of branding. This gentleman is informed not only on the history of branding in the American West, but can tell you all about the branding of camels in Egypt and the marking of cattle long before Christ.

"Building my collection of irons, many of which are rare, has called for much reading, correspondence, interviewing, buying, trading, and, yes—occasionally stealing! Of course there are scores of American irons I lack and would love to possess, but most of the ones I am genuinely eager to obtain now are on ranches of foreign lands."

The Hale collection is not limited to stamping and running irons. There is also a library of books, clippings, pamphlets, manuscripts, and pictures which deal with the cattle industry and which emphasize branding in particular. Almost any sort of object is treasured there, if it has to do with branding or range heraldry in any form. The Hale house is decorated with countless objects and "souvenirs", ranging from branded draperies and shoes to the branded door from the men's toilet in an old-time saloon.

John Hale was hunting quail in the Tonto Basin country above Roosevelt Dam in Arizona one time, when he came onto an old deserted school house. The roof was mostly gone, the windows held no panes, some of the wall boards were missing. But on the floor inside was a hardwood desk top of the type used on pupils' desks from about the turn of the century onward. John brushed off the dirt and dust and studied the children's carvings on this old piece of wood. Then he carried it through ten miles of wilderness to his car and drove home with it. It is today a valued piece among his collections, because its surface is carved not with boys' and girls' initials, comic faces, or aimless scrolls, but with a dozen or more cattle brands.

Famous in Arizona cattle history is the Double Circle carved there; the ranch is still one of the state's largest. Near it is cut the Flying H of Pecos McFadden. Now gone but recorded there in wood is the Lazy Y 4 of the Kleinmans. Levi Grantham sears Open A Cross on the ribs of his cattle now. Cows bearing Tex Barkley's Quarter Circle U graze on the lower slopes of Superstition Mountain, as do the Y Slash Z cattle of the Weeks outfit. Well known in the White Mountains is the Broken Arrow. Bernard Hughes has replaced the Diamond brand with a Circle Bar, but his ranch is still known as the Diamond. Largest in the upper Tonto region is the Bar T Bar of Tremaines. And some boy from each of these ranches in the long ago put his daddy's brand there on the desk top in the isolated mountain school. Near the center of the board is a brand which the carver proudly claimed by cutting his name under it, thus:

D O C

This gave John Hale a clue. He remembered that George Cline was the cattle king of the Tonto region, and that Dr. Benjamin Baker Moeur, who later became governor of Arizona, once delivered a baby on the Cline ranch; the baby was named for Dr. Moeur and nicknamed Doc. John wrote Doc Cline to call when he was next in town, and when Doc, now a grown man, came by and saw the old desk top he almost shed tears.

"Yes, sir," Doc declared, "I remember putting that T Turkey Track there, when I was just a kid. I know all of the other carvers, too. I mean I did then. We had grand times at that school. Never had a student body of more than ten at a time, but it was our school.

"I remember we got the teacher to omit the two short recess periods and make the lunch hour that much longer, and this gave us time at lunch to go to a nearby canyon infested with several big pack rats' nests. With the aid of dogs and snares we caught many of the rats alive, played they were cattle, and branded them with a piece of hot wire. I had over a hundred in my herd.

"A few years after I had finished that school, when I was grown, I was riding through that canyon and I noticed an old gray patriarch rat sitting on a rock. I shot him, and you will never know how thrilled I was when I examined him and found him to be a 'steer' still carrying my T Turkey Track brand."

It is such supplementary items as this desk top, with such "pedigrees" behind them, which make the Hale collection one of inestimable value.

In the high red rocky mountains of Arizona are many relics of a forgotten people who lived in locations stranger than any other men have ever known. No one knows exactly how long ago they lived there. Present Indians refer to them simply as The People Who Were Here Before. Whence they came, and where they went, and when and why, are matters for archaeological conjecture and guessing. All we really do know is that these folk, peaceful agriculturalists, were cave dwellers who did not dwell in any convenient caves they could find but erected clan houses and mansions of masonry in cave-niches eroded in the sheer sides of cliffs, and contrived long precarious stairways and ladders to get down to their crops in the valleys.

If you have never seen the remains of an ancient cliff-dwelling you have difficulty envisioning such a site. Imagine that the Rockefeller Center in New York or the Merchandise Mart in Chicago was a cliff of solid rock, running not quite straight up but overhanging or leaning over space somewhat. Then up about the thirtieth or fortieth floor, imagine a gash or niche cut in this cliff by wind and rain and time, a shelf-like hole large enough to contain a modern five-room cottage and its flower garden.

In just such eagles' eyries those ancients established their homes. They didn't squat and live like beasts. They dug finger and toe holds zigzagging up the cliff wall, laboriously carried up mud and poles and reeds for thatching, excavated back into the mountain-side a bit more (they had not metals, only the crudest tools), and erected solid houses that sometimes had three and four stories and dozens of rooms, built so well that many are still in excellent condition to this day.

A few modern highways have curved close to such cliff dwellings, so that with short detours or even with field glasses travelers can look up at the past. Few people actually bother to climb up to them because the exertion is great; they are content to stand down on the flat land and gaze upward in awe. Some of these cliff dwellings are national monuments, others are just isolated exhibits known to explorers and archaeologists.

One day a few years ago a motion picture actor deserted Hollywood for a short time and came into Arizona to hunt grizzly bear. He had ample money, good health, plenty of time, so he outfitted himself for quite a trip. Four days out from the last country trading post, in extremely wild and rugged country, his field glasses revealed such a high cliff dwelling as those described.

Nothing would do but what he must go to it. The guides with him said they had never seen the spot before, and that it probably was new to the eyes of modern man. The actor's curiosity and interest mounted as they rode along. He couldn't get up to the base of the cliff without some very difficult travel, and when he did get there he could find no way whatsoever to get up the overhanging wall. The cliff was defiant— just as it had been centuries ago to the enemies of the brown people who lived up there, and who probably came raiding. The actor tried to find the secret stair. He did find a few foot-

and hand-holds, but the ancient ladders had rotted away. All he could see was a two-story building high in the niche shelf, with windows and doors and poles still showing.

In his equipment, however, was considerable rope, and since he was known as an athletic actor anyway, he thought to do a sensational thing. He worked his guides and himself and their rope away around to the top of the cliff, slid down a rope, swung out and in, out and in, out and in, until he finally landed on the cliff dwelling porch. Then for an hour he explored.

He was of course an intelligent man, and he took notes on what he saw. Two mummies, of old women; dried up there in the arid Arizona air, back away from any sunshine. Remains of several fires. Pottery. Shards and artifacts of several kinds. Some decayed fabrics. Arrowheads. A pile of corn cobs. Dust and dirt. A silence broken only by ghostly winds. And—peculiar inscriptions prominent on an inside wall.

He explored all the eight rooms and made careful study of the inscriptions. As he mused there he felt a mounting elation; unless his guess was badly wrong, this hitherto unknown cliff dwelling held a link with ancient Asia. Some of the characters in the wall inscription suggested forms in the Arabic alphabet, although in general they made no sense. The actor studied them minutely. He would hasten back to civilization, announce his discovery and get national headlines for having made a significant contribution to science. (A motion picture actor can use national headlines any day.)

He carried out that hasty plan up to a certain point. He did forget about hunting grizzlies and proceed back to Phoenix at once, where he told his story to a distinguished archaeologist. The actor was known to the scientist by reputation. Their meeting was an impressive one. (The actor's press agent carefully saw to that.) The archaeologist arranged to go at once to the isolated cliff dwelling, and the press agent arranged to withhold the news until he could make a big news break with photographs of both men actually on the scene. A newsreel camera, too, went along this time. Guiding this second and very impressive expedition were three efficient but rather silent cowboys, from a ranch which backed up into that mountain range. Theirs was the honor of accompanying the very first white man—a noted actor—ever to set foot in this important archaeological find. They stood to get their pictures in the newspapers and on the movie screen—reflected glory.

When after great labor and expense the party finally got into the cliff dwelling, the actor led them straight to the inscriptions. He pointed gracefully to them—poised just right while the camera lights flashed—and the archaeologist walked over to see them at close range. The other men then came near.

Not the archaeologist, but one of the squinting cowboy guides spoke first through that dramatic hush, however.

"Why them ain't no old pre-historical stuff, gentle-men," he drawled. "Them's just some cow brands."

They all stared at him, transfixed.

"You mean—?" The actor was pale.

"Yais, sir. That'n there, it's th' Double J Bar. And that next un's a Cross S, and this'n is a Broke Arrer, and this'n here, it's McFadden's Flyin' H. It's just been a bunch of cowboys come up here every now 'n' then, snoopin' around. They're likely to leave their tracks like this anywhar."

CHAPTER XI

ON HUMAN HIDE

IF you are one of those hardy investigators who are never satisfied with second-hand information, then go ahead now and try fire branding from the receiving end.

You can, if you are that enthusiastic, take a regulation cattle branding iron, heat it and slap it onto your flesh. You will live to regret it, for you will have contributed nothing to human knowledge and accomplished nothing else to justify the suffering. Since your experiment will be only a stunt anyway, try a piece of small stiff wire. Wire can glow red hot, burn you so as to hurt like the devil, and leave a very permanent scar.

Twist the wire around gracefully and make the brand design into a flat plane so that it can be stamped on quickly. You will never have nerve enough to do a running iron brand either on yourself or on your friend, so acute the pain will be, unless you are an extreme sadist. Best choose a hidden spot about your body because the scar, to your chagrin, probably will not be in the smooth design in which you made the burn. It should be located for convenience in bandaging, too, because almost surely you will have a miserable sore there for several weeks. It may even become infected and be a prolonged nuisance and agony, finally claiming your very life, in which case your relatives doubtless will be saddened at your passing, but the remainder of the world will be better off for having rid itself of another fool.

Voluntary fire branding is by no means common, but it is not unknown. Crackpots of various sorts have branded themselves since away back, when motivated possibly by something which merits our sympathies, but the sum of them can be dismissed as unimportant. Much more interesting are the conditions under which human beings have been fire-branded against their will. In this category must come the members of fraternities and lodges whose clanship is proclaimed forever by unsightly scars.

Dr. Harvey Howard of St. Louis, Missouri, was exploring in the wilds of Tibet when Chinese bandits captured him. The bandits, unaccustomed to a white victim, stripped him and examined him minutely as a preliminary to shooting him, and in doing so discovered a peculiar Greek letter brand on his arm. Bound by the taboos of their superstitions, they refused to execute any man with such a mysterious mark on his body, and so his life was spared. The scar was one from Dr. Howard's Nu Sigma Nu initiation rites, and while he doubtless came home more enthusiastic than ever for fraternities and their childish mumbo-jumbo, this is the only authentic case we can find wherein a fraternity brand actually served any practical good.

Youths in college, and a few older men with minds still undeveloped, like to prove by fire branding that they can "take it". They may even know in advance of initiation into the frat or lodge that they will be subjected to the burn, and thus it can be called voluntary. Most of them, however, rebel at the actual application of the iron. Many college kids, it can be said in their favor, are unaware that they must be branded until they actually face the ordeal, but they develop a certain pride in it immediately after the initiation is over. We do not know of any important lodges that do fire branding. Various chapters of the

Ku Klux Klan, as of the twentieth century, introduced fiery branding as well as fiery crosses into its rituals, but it never did sit well with the members. It is one thing to be impressed deeply with one's undying loyalty to a Cause while inside a sheet under a fiery cross on a hillside at midnight, but when the burned badge of initiation still hurts tomorrow and the next day, and festers so as to require a doctor's care, the Cause can go hang. Certain other lesser lodges and secret societies for male adults, including a few for negroes in the South and at least one for negroes in New York City, brand their novices to impress them with the importance (if any) of their joining, but mostly these seem to be sporadic rituals conceived by men who for one reason or another couldn't get into the higher class organizations.

Most of the fire branding of human beings has been done on the hides of criminals and slaves. We cannot say when the first criminal or slave was branded, nor how. Early Romans branded the letter F on thieves. For a century or so prior to 1636, the letter F (for *fraymaker*) was branded on the chests of street fighters arrested in England. During the same period England also branded gipsies and tramps, using the letter V, for *vagrant*. Galley slaves were branded in France until the turn of the nineteenth century, and the French also burned a *fleur de lys* on the left shoulders of prostitutes and adulterers. Early Greeks branded their slaves with a delta.

In England and in the English colonies in America, laymen who were convicted of a felony after claiming benefit of clergy, were branded on the left thumb; women guilty of simple larceny were burned in the hand, until later legislation provided that they be branded on the cheek. Colonial penalties included the well known scarlet letter sewed upon the clothes, but less known is the fact that the culprit was burned on the face if the scarlet letter was removed. The death penalty gave way to fire branding for certain offenses in Connecticut in 1637. Branding is also mentioned there in the code of 1769. Early Massachusetts burned an A on the forehead of certain offenders.

None of the records are very detailed, but there is definite evidence that quite a number of male and female "witches" of our shameful colonial days were branded with fire. Of course the more vicious practitioners of witchcraft were dunked in water or put in stocks or even burned alive. Possibly the lesser ones were subjected to the branding, just as a warning to themselves and to those whom they might victimize.

Negro slavery in America of course brought fire branding with it. Not all slaves were branded, but many thousands of them were. In their case, branding was often more for identification than for punishment; they were labeled indelibly so that their owners might know them, exactly as cows were and are branded. This branding usually was done on the African coast. One authority on slave practices says, "If the purchasers were the Dutch Company, the slaves were promptly branded to prevent their being confused in the crowd before being carried on shipboard." We can only hope that a small iron was used.

The white folk in America looked with horror on negro branding just for identification, and so even the heartless slave owners did little of it over here, lest the value of their property be depreciated thereby. But many white men felt that branding as punishment was just and effective. It probably was more effective than just. It was used after acts of gross disobedience, for running away, for burglary, or for murdering a fellow slave. The intense pain of fire naturally was a deterrent from further crime. A slave owner couldn't punish a slave by execution, for some heinous crime such as murder, any more than he could execute a bull for goring another bull to death. Both the bull and the negro were too valuable to be destroyed. Fire branding therefore served a genuine need, under standards of that day.

We can find no practice of enforced branding of human beings in the world today if we except the practices of warfare which—praise God—usually are but passing orgies. When the Italians were raping Ethiopia, at least one reputable authority reported that the Ethiopians were fire-branding their own deserters when captured. Red-hot irons were drawn in lines from forehead to chin, around the sides of the face. The Japanese also devised some particularly brutal methods of torturing their Chinese victims in their undeclared war, including the use of hot irons. But these things may be dismissed simply as normal; when man is determined to go to war in the first place, fire branding is thoroughly in harmony with his warped brain.

One of the objects which man in his male superiority has always felt that he "possessed" has been his woman. She has been more (or perhaps we should say less) than a helpmeet and lover; she has been personal property, sometimes even today she is virtually a slave. Accordingly, it is no new thought for man to brand her.

The late Will C. Barnes, whom we have already quoted as an authority on the American cattle industry and on branding lore, told of seeing a fire brand put on a woman's thigh. While a young cowpuncher, Will was assisting a prominent Mormon stockman brand some calves in northern Arizona. Some of the women of the household were watching the procedure. Their expressions of sympathy for the poor calves irritated the rancher and he ordered the women to go back to the ranch house. One woman, failing to obey the command, slipped around and watched through the rails at a different part of the corral; but the fiery-tempered Mormon detected her presence, grabbed a red-hot branding iron, jumped the fence and gave chase. The woman shrieked in holy terror. Handicapped in that era by many skirts, she tripped and fell, exposing part of one leg. The rancher lifted the skirts still higher and slapped down the hot iron, branding her forever with a two-inch circle right on the thigh.

"Bully Bob" Bascom, who made and lost several fortunes at gambling in Reno, Nevada, after getting rich in the cattle business, first came into notoriety when he had his brand made into gold *conchos* and set on his horse's bridle, then shot a man for trying to steal the bridle. The brand looked like this:

People knew that it stood for Robert Bascom, the R reversed, connected with the B. It was called the R B Connected, or sometimes the Bully Bob Brand because Bob was unquestionably bullish. He used to get drunk, step out onto the Reno sidewalk and roar, "WHA-A-A-AH, I'm a two-legged hellion with studhorse in my groins, and I'll kill any son of a —— that says I ain't!" He wasn't exaggerating.

The state's best looking scarlet lady fell for him. Her name —that is, the name she used—was Suzette Adair. She was as young and fiery as Bully Bob himself. In a purely biological sense they made ideal mates, and Bob decided at their first meeting that she would henceforth be his property and his alone.

Suzette liked that state of affairs for a few months, until the inevitable happened. Another handsome man came along, offering the novelty of being new. Suzette entertained him, and when Bully Bob found it out he went berserk. He ran the other man far past the city limits, leaping just beyond pistol range, and came back to Suzette. Suzette sought to pacify him with her wiles, but Bully Bob snatched a golden *concho* from his bridle, held it with fireplace tongs and heated it, then branded her with it. Next day he married her and dared any other man ever to touch her again. She was probably the only woman in history ever to be branded with an "iron" of gold.

Olive and Mary Ann Oatman, aged sixteen and seven respectively, were traveling with their family in an ox wagon across southern Arizona in 1851 when Apache Indians appeared. The savages murdered all but the two girls and a brother, and left the brother for dead. The girls were taken into captivity. Their history is now a beloved western saga, recounting especially the brother's efforts to find and rescue them. After some years Olive was returned to the society of whites. She gave a terrible account of her baby sister's death and of her own tortures, and she bore brand marks on her chin. The Apaches, and later the Mohaves, had learned a trick from the palefaces and branded their property for identification.

Mrs. Carlos Gil Gonzales of New Mexico came in to Santa Fe for an appendicitis operation when she was almost fifty years of age, and the nurses and physician discovered this scar on her abdomen:

The nurses were appalled. "Why ever were you branded?" they asked.

"Carlos, he brand me," she replied, quite seriously. "He brand everytheeng. Thee cows, thee horses, thee goat, thee cheeldren, everytheeng. Eet ees hees brand, no?"

The lady saw nothing amiss. Indeed, she was obviously proud of her identifying mark.

By far the majority of all authentic accounts of the branding of women, however, slip quickly into the category of humor or of dude doings.

CHAPTER XII

SYNTHETIC HERALDRY

A DUDE, says the cowboy, is a New Yorker who asks questions. One stock question is, "Which side of a cow do you put the brand on?" The cowboy's stock answer is: "The outside." Their little dialogue is more significant than silly. It reveals much of the character of each.

The typical dude has changed radically in the past twenty-five or so years. The dude of 1910 has gone the way of the Texas Longhorn steer; a few of him are to be found but mostly he is a museum piece. The modern dude is a smart and smart-looking individual, a whole lot more valuable than his predecessor, just as the modern steer is a heavier, more valuable critter than the old rangy Longhorn. Yesterday's dude was a sap with a high white collar. Today's dude is an intelligent city resident with money in his pants.

The dude strain was bred up rapidly from that crude early species with the phenomenal development of the automobile. In the old days dudes came West because they were running away from a sheriff or a fiancée or a family disgrace, or were steaming with a zeal for research. They were tolerated, but were never too welcome, despite the realities of western hospitality. The modern dude not only is welcome, he is aggressively courted and enticed; partly because herding him is more profitable than herding steers, and partly because ranchers are more broad-minded about him, recognizing him as a sociable, sensible fellow—often a distinguished fellow—with whom it is highly pleasurable and beneficial to rub brains. He is an envoy from the East where men are more gregarious than are western cows. He brings talk of The Other Half. He opens mental channels, reveals cultural horizons, in return for a chance to view some new kinds of scenery from a horse's back. Part of this new scenery which he seeks is the ranch brand. He likes to think of himself as branded with the range traditions and legends, likes to feel he is part of western heraldry, likes to ride and work and play with the saddled knights themselves. Because he can afford the time and cost, and because automobiles have enabled him to erase the great barrier of distance, he is coming to the West in ever increasing numbers. He is a distinctly new social entity on the American scene.

Life magazine a few months ago stated that twelve thousand easterners go to dude ranches every summer, spending over three million dollars. That may be a fair estimate, for summer. But the big dude "draw" is to the Southwest for *winter*. During September in small groups, like milch cows ambling homeward across a pasture, dudes and dudettes and their dudelings (children) begin drifting to the warm desert region along our Mexican frontier; immediately after the Christmas celebrations are ended in the cold cities, these folk start rushing in like great cattle herds cascading over a hill. Special trains have to be run to such sunny cities as San Antonio, El Paso, Tucson, Phoenix and San Diego, and on the regular trains a Pullman berth in winter comes only to the lucky early applicant. Highway checking stations at state lines become rushed, and airplane seats are likely to be all filled. Those five cities, especially the first four named, are distributing points for the dude herds. At the railroad stations and air terminals special buses and other cars meet the dudes to haze them right on out to the ranch resorts. The wary dudes who elect to go to the city hotels and "look around" a bit first may be embarrassed to find all hotel rooms filled, even those hotels whose rooms cost fifteen to thirty-five dollars a day, saddle horses extra. To all of these migrants, however, snow becomes only a headline on an Associated Press article. The realities of life become a big Stetson, a loud shirt, tight pants, boots, spurs, lariat ropes, prodigious appetites, horses, cows, brands and branding irons.

It is now unwise to say just when and where the dude ranching idea originated, because three or four sections are claiming the honor, if honor it be. (The matter is controversial!) Eaton Brothers in Wyoming are said to have entertained the first dudes for pay; but so is a ranch in New Mexico said to have done it first. A great many stern old-timers still resent the intrusion of human stock on the western ranges; they feel that a rancher who substitutes dudes for steers has traded his very soul for money. And it may be that he has. It may be that dude herding presages the end of genuine range heraldry. The city dudes are gradually but surely engulfing the West with their damnable "efficiency", and such fine things as chivalry and knight-errantry usually flee out the window when Yankee efficiency busts in the door. There's no telling what may happen to branding when it becomes as heartless and mechanical as chain stores.

The typical dude family to date, however, is still glowing from the thrill of discovery. The sheer difference of life on a ranch is enough to overwhelm them for a while. Also they are paying fees of twenty-five to a hundred dollars a person a week, depending on the elegance of the ranch they have chosen, and they want their money's worth. The rancher and his dressed-up cowboys are just as anxious to give them their money's worth, and so in the end everybody is satisfied. Rodeos, *fiestas*, *bailes*, hunting trips, fishing sprees, barbecues, Indian ceremonials, will be enjoyed before the get-western interlude is over. The dudes plunge in to be good sports and enjoy themselves as much as they can. In no time at all they feel a love for *their* ranch; in a very few days they have acquired the contagious loyalty to *their* brand, just as a college freshman quickly acquires a fierce loyalty for his school. Dudes have been known to fight with words, fists and even guns in defense of what they considered the good name of the home ranch brand, feeling and demonstrating even more fiercely than a stolid cow ranny would do. Perhaps this is a good sign.

The president of a New York bank, ordered by his doctor to go out West and rest up his high blood pressure, rested it by personally applying the Forks-of-the-Road brand to more than a thousand cows. He wielded the stamping iron at first rather sheepishly when his host the rancher grinned and invited him to. He got by with it pretty good. Next calf dragged up found him waiting over it with another hot iron, and the boys just let him keep on. He made a right good ranch "hand"—he whose daily income was almost a thousand dollars. The men working beside him there got a dollar and a half a day, but they all liked each other. They probably never thought about it, but they were performing in an exclusively American way and their democracy was a priceless thing.

The banker found that although his appetite had been expensively finicky back on Park Avenue, it seemed to go on stampede in Arizona, enabling him to devour unbelievable quantities of fresh beef cooked on a green stick held in his own hand over the branding fire. A connoisseur of breads theretofore, he learned quickly to eat heavy dutch-oven biscuits made by a bewhiskered cook not too careful as to dust and grit. He learned to cuss a little, cowboy fashion. He learned how to roll a cigarette from a package of Bull Durham tobacco, tightening the drawstring again with the aid of his teeth, how to light it and smoke it and never miss a word of the long story he was telling. When he finally reached the climax or point of his story, and heard the cowpokes mutter "Well, I'll be damned!" he knew it was not sarcasm but appreciation. When they started calling him "Ed" instead of "Mr. Dunbar",[1] and began telling him brand histories and legends, and began teaching him how to weave a riata from rawhide or from maguey fibres, and began teaching him to speak Mexican, the banker knew he had achieved a station in life which he could never achieve back home.

Next day he wired his secretaries to sell out his eastern holdings because he had come West for good. The ranch hadn't been any too prosperous of late anyway; its owner had been whipped down by the depression. Mr. Dunbar—Ed Dunbar—bought it for a fair price, cash. As soon as he could he drove in to the capitol at Phoenix and had ownership of the Forks-in-the-Road brand transferred to his name. Then he went by the Porter saddlery, had a Mexican worker there burn special invitations on cowhide for him. The lettering was an invitation to visit the Forks-in-the-Road Ranch, and the rectangles of leather were to go air mail to twenty-five erstwhile cronies of Edward Harrison Dunbar, Esq. But the ranch owner himself

[1] Not his real name, although the instance is real.

took the red-hot electric needle from the Mexican and personally burned on his new signature:

Ed Dunbar

Of course very few of the dudes are absorbed as quickly or as happily into range life as Ed Dunbar was. A great many women and girls come out with the open or hidden intent of catching a man, the generic cowboy having through fiction and screen dramas corralled all the glamor they can possibly imagine. In point of statistical fact, few of these predatory dudettes ever actually marry cowboys, although some right swift romances do materialize, and a bespectacled gal may acquire a fixation for that long lanky fellow with the trick rope. Knowing this proclivity of his female guests, the dude rancher is likely to pick his cowboys for their profiles and their ability to croon with a guitar under the moonlight, rather than for their skill at castrating, de-horning, and removing screw worms. Last year's annual convention of the western dude ranchers association admitted openly that its principal drawing power was "romance", and that its members needed to hire better looking male riders. Unfortunately this admission got into the newspapers and caused the ranchers no little embarrassment.

The list of distinguished people who have seen through the dust and manure of cattle raising to discover the heraldry of the range, and so become addicts of ranch living or at least of ranch vacations, is a very long one. One of America's most popular fiction writers, Clarence Budington Kelland, suffered a breakdown of his trailer car while heading for the Pacific coast. Forced to rest by the side of the highway in Arizona, he struck up an acquaintance with cow folk, with cow talk and horse talk and grass talk and brand talk, and forthwith pulled up his eastern roots. His new home is a ranch near Phoenix—a dudish ranch, but a ranch—and his latest best seller is a historical romance about a pretty girl rancher, titled *Arizona*.

Bud Kelland is a homely, homey sort of man who admittedly is not the least bit "literary"—his popular *Arizona* is a mess by scholastic standards of literature—but at the other end of the scale is J. B. Priestley, of London and points east and west, who spends most of his winters in Arizona. His opus was called *Midnight on the Desert* and it became a fast seller too, although men who live by the saddle couldn't understand much of it. One old whanghide cowpoke who tried to read it put it down and said, truthfully, "He throws too much dust." Priestley didn't care; he wasn't writing for the ranch folk, he was writing about them.

General Pershing owes the latter years of his life not to city hospitals but to southwestern ranch sunshine. Edna Ferber gets away from it all by going very exclusively dudish at the most expensive dude ranch in the world. ("It costs five dollars to spit, out there.") Numerous other big names have been registered there, as of course have the inevitable screen stars and others whose distinction is the synthetic variety begotten of dollars and ballyhoo. One and all they are pretty good people. They are not half as haughty as poor folk imagine them to be. Some have a genuine aristocracy, but aristocracy is just democracy in full dress. They have all heard about and now want to share the legends of rangeland, the heraldry of the plains.

For four dollars and ninety-five cents—which is mighty close to five dollars—the most exclusive department store at Phoenix will send you a "tailored playsuit of linen, lined and fitted, white background with brands of red, blue or brown." Modeled by the pretty college co-ed in the advertisement it looks about like a swim suit except that it isn't quite so form-fitting. Anyway the next picture shows the same lovely girl wearing a "perfect fitting satin lastex bathing suit in concord blue with silvery white brands, pastel beige with brown brands, or white with wedgwood blue brands." The price, if you're interested, is ten ninety-five, so obviously it is cheaper to play western out of water. In addition there are branding iron shirts, branded bush coats and slacks, and branded handkerchiefs, dresses, shoes, hats, purses, belts, neckerchiefs, anklets, bracelets, and scanty pants. Each item is of exquisite daintiness and beauty, and each is stamped with a selection of famous cattle brands. When these clever fashions were introduced during the Phoenix world-championship rodeo a few winters ago, they "took" instantly and spread throughout the West, then on into the East and into Europe.

This is precisely the sort of thing that delights the average dude and dudette. They do not have the time, ordinarily, to steep themselves in range traditions, they want their brand heraldry predigested and served to them in quickly assimilable form. What more delightful way to go western than to don an outfit all covered with brands? Especially since the brands are copies of genuine ones that are registered and often being burned on cattle today. And have fascinating stories behind them.

Branding iron fabrics and fashions were created by Barry Goldwater, who promptly berated himself for not having thought up the idea sooner. Imitators with other western patterns followed in a veritable cascade, some to meet with very good success for a few weeks. The cartoon patterns, the Mexican designs, the dress goods with mountain and desert scenery printed on, all enjoyed good sales. These, however, were mostly accepted as are any other passing fads and fashions, after which interest subsided. The branding material went right on through with a steady sale.

When the fabric with brands on it came out in heavy linens and crashes, it instantly became popular as drapery material. An increasing number of city homes in the West are of the rancho style of architecture, and this brand material fitted in perfectly for curtains and even for upholstery. A few builders pasted the material right onto ceilings and walls, replacing wall paper. In time some enterprising manufacturer will of course introduce brands on wall paper, if it hasn't already been done.

Because the brand designs are not gaudy, because they are symbolic as well as decorative, because they are deeply rooted into the western consciousness, the fashion is almost certain to endure. The annual dude stampede of course adds impetus each season, so that the home residents feel that their branded shirts, dresses, shoes et cetera are perpetually in style, as indeed they are. The cut of the dresses will vary from year to year, the selection and placing of the brands can be changed, but the idea need not be. This much has already been demonstrated.

Most of the attractive guest registry books, photograph albums, and general scrapbooks seen in the smart western shops last year were bound not with cloth or board, but with plain tan strap leather covered with burned brands. These things retailed at prices ranging from two to fifteen dollars. Leather is not expensive, paper is even less so, and the rawhide thong which binds the book is worth maybe a dime. But the whole thing has a look of high quality, and for that matter *is* of high quality, which is what matters in merchandising. The exclusive customer can purchase a book bound in blank leather and have a personal selection of brands burned on.

The authors of this book have in their living rooms parchment lampshades of translucent white, adorned with famous cattle brands. A guest has yet to enter either home and not exclaim over the novelty and beauty of these shades. The stand of one lamp is wrapped and laced with cowhide, hair still on.

The drawer pulls of dressers and chests in western furniture are likely to be leather straps burned with several cattle brands. They are pretty and practical as well.

The bedspreads in western homes may be of the patented branding iron fabric, or may be of home-designed material with the brands sewed on. Of course, women on cattle ranches have been sewing their own and their friends' brands onto their quilts for at least a hundred years; some of these are of exceptional artistry. A common quilt design is that in which the home ranch brand is about a foot wide in the center, with smaller squares carrying other brands around it. Beauty of course depends on mother's ingenuity and rag bag. Dudes who slept under one such homemade quilt in California were so impressed that they offered to buy it. The embarrassed ranch lady didn't want to sell. When they kept on admiring it she "up and give it to 'em," and later the grateful dudes sent her a silver tea service from back East. She will never have any use for the tea service— ranches just don't go in for tea parties—but she was so proud of it she cried, and she doubtless will hand it on down to her granddaughter. The teapot and the creamer and the sugar bowl and the silver tray all were engraved with her ranch brand.

Now it was more or less natural that, inasmuch as a cattle ranch always brands its stock, a dude ranch should feel the urge and the need to brand its stock, too. A burned K Bar 9 on a steer's rump is an advertisement at market for the K Bar 9 ranch and, just as any other trademark has publicity value in merchandising, will build up a reputation for K Bar 9 cows. Some meat retailers even capitalize on famous brands and advertise that they sell meat raised under specific ranch brands; as early as 1860 "Pete Kitchen's Beef and Ham" brought a premium on the market at Tucson over any competitor's meat. So, what could be done to brand the modern dudes, and send them back home carrying an advertisement for the ranch where they had visited?

It wasn't sufficient to give them little gadgets or souvenirs. A lapel pin brand might be worn for a time, or a bracelet or ring. But these become nuisances, are lost, mislaid, forgotten. And aren't very clever anyway. How could a brand be actually *burned* onto a dude or dudette, into the very skin, as it is on a cow? The literal hot iron or chemical obviously was out of the question.

Dudettes themselves solved the problem. One week a dozen or so really pretty and shapely girls witnessed the cowboys at branding work on the I O U ranch. They asked an old cow hand about it.

"Yais, ma'am," he told the spokesman, "we allus hev to brand th' calves, so's we can look at 'em and tell whose they are."

Forthwith the girls went off to bask in the sunshine and a few days later exhibited their own calves proudly showing white I O U brands against deep tan. The rancher viewed the legs with combined embarrassment and delight.

You can brand yourself, if you like, without ever going west

of the Mississippi River, or even west of the Hudson. The sun
out West is likely to be a bit more potent because it has to go
through less moisture and smoke, but if you can arrange even
a rooftop or a fire escape where the sunbeams play, you can
play at dude ranching. Children especially will enjoy the
branding stunt.

Cut a brand, any brand, about two or three inches high, from
ordinary adhesive tape. Stick it on your leg or arm and expose
it to sunshine. Take only five minutes or so the first day, ten
minutes the next, twenty minutes the next, and so on until you
can stand an hour or two of it without blistering your skin.
Leave the adhesive on all the time, night and day, replacing with
a fresh one as necessary. It won't be long until you have a bright
burned "scar" just like any range heifer or bull, except that
yours (fortunately!) won't be as permanent.

CHAPTER XIII

FUN AND FANCY FREE

MR. PITHECANTHROPUS ERECTUS, who had been studiously minding what he would have called his own business, was nevertheless bowed down considerably with worry. It seems that the female child reared over beyond the next mountain had grown remarkably of late, had replaced angular elbows and knotted knees with curves and had—by George!—miraculously developed not the long straight black hair of most cave dwellers, but curly golden hair! Mr. Erectus wasn't the only man who had discovered these things, wherefore his worry.

He squatted now with feet flat and his knees up near his ears, scowling at the fire there before him. He had a spotted leopard-skin around his middle, so he pulled it astern and sat down on it, an early dawning of the love of luxury. He scowled some more, and jerked the head off a rabbit he had killed, sucked its blood and ate most of it raw, and roasted some of it just for fun. He was trying to figure some way to beat hell out of young John Barrelchest, who had a cave up on Sky Peak and who was also trying to claim Golden Hair. In fact John had been noising it around everywhere that Golden Hair was his, and our hero didn't like it.

He sulked there for half an hour and, because it was cold that morning, he presently turned his posterior to the fire to warm it also. Then, as a man in love will, he became absent minded; the leopard-skin flapped onto a live coal, blaze skimmed up it and stabbed Mr. Erectus on the left rear cheek.

"OUW!" shrieked Mr. Erectus, or whatever the prehistoric word for *ouw* might have been.

He put out the blaze on his leopard-skin easily enough, then squatted over a pool of water to study his burn. Mirrored there was an angry red spot. He knew it would be there forever as a scar, because he had burned his hand once years ago and it still showed.

"Aha!" he cried then, thinking for the first time in human existence.

He jumped up and grabbed his club and trotted away toward the mountain. You see, he had stopped worrying; he had figured out a way to thwart John Barrelchest and proclaim to the world that Golden Hair was Mrs. Erectus.

He high-tailed it over the mountain, bopped Golden Hair affectionately and effectively over the cranium with his club, dragged her lovingly home and sat down to his task. He heated a long sharp rock in his fire and knelt beside her.

He thought at first to monogram her smack on the left rear cheek, where he had himself been burned, but when he inspected the area there he decided it was too doggone beautiful to be harmed. He looked next at her breast, but the contours there were defiant in their beauty also. He looked at her face speculatively, and she smiled at him through the yellow ringlets against which zephyrs were playing.

"Shucks!" said Mr. Erectus, blushing; or whatever the prehistoric word for *shucks* might have been. He just couldn't touch her face with a hot rock.

So, he looked down at her lower legs. Because she was a

cave lady and had to use them too much, the lower legs were not very delicate and shapely, and wouldn't be for at least another nine million years. "Unh!" grunted Mr. Erectus, satisfied, and seared her there with his initials, a neat three-inch monogram:

Ǝ

He knew darn well then that John Barrelchest couldn't claim her any more, nor any other man, because she was marked for him and him alone.

And that, ladies and gentleman, is a record of the first branding done in this world. Selah.

Two things have stood out prominently in the character of the typical American cowboy—his utter self-reliance, and his sense of humor. Without either he could not have existed.

When Curly Bill walked eight miles back to the ranch house, carrying his saddle, he *grinned* when he admitted through his fatigue that his horse had slipped away from him in the night. He could see it as a joke on himself.

When Ed Taliaferro, trying to brand a yearning bull single-handed, was kicked into a pile of soft cow dung, he got up cussing but he was able to grin when he went to the windmill trough to wash himself. His misfortune cost the boss several dollars because fifteen men who witnessed it had to take time off to whoop and holler and razz poor Ed. And the boss himself thought it so funny that he told about it in the bank lobby when he went to town next Saturday.

When the new boy from town came out to work at his first ranch job, they served him mountain oysters cooked for supper, and watched him turn green when they finally told him what they were. In point of fact, the meat was delicious and thoroughly wholesome, but the young fellow had to have his education in the matter.

Now you, who are sheltered by skyscrapers rather than by mountain peaks, guarded by policemen rather than by cactus thorns, may not understand that kind of humor. It may sound crude and distinctly un-funny to you.

The only answer is that it wasn't meant for you. You are not their kind, and the ranch folk much prefer that you go right on living in the city where they can sell you their beef. Your kind of humor is the sophisticated repartee of the cocktail lounge, the subtle dialogue, *double entendre*, expletive and invective of the ultra-modern stage. But of the two types, the cowboy's humor is the more honest. His is earthy and elemental, spontaneous and good.

Practically anything having to do with sex organs, male or female, human or animal, is considered funny to the cowboy. To a lesser extent are the machinations of the digestive tract and elimination system considered humorous. Don't ask why; they just are. A cowboy is very likely to be "dirty mouthed" even though he is extremely kind hearted and loyal. He is likely to talk filth and think purity. That's the man of him, the outdoorsy unrefined man.

These traits are reflected in his cattle brands. A great many really good brand stories cannot be included here for the simple reason that they will not bear being put into print. But come out to the bunkhouse with us some night after supper, squat on your haunches and lean back against the wall while Shorty and Curly and Ed and Wes and old man Merridew spin their spiciest yarns. Some of the brand histories that are a little off color have achieved respectability. Ed Stamm, who was Arizona state veterinarian for sixteen years, fire-marked his cattle with this peculiar heraldic crest:

$$2 \sim P$$

It isn't peculiar unless you have an equally peculiar sense of humor. At a glance it appears to be just another typically unimaginative brand, but it has been used to make many a thousand girls blush, and a few thousand bashful young men as well. If you can't translate it, study your lesson back on page 42 for a cue.

Best of the yarns, best of the lore of range heraldry in general, is to be heard when day's work is done and men have relaxed, preferably around the white-red coals and coffee pot of an outdoor fire. Making no attempt at exhaustive coverage or at weaving any sort of continuity into them, we will present the following miscellany of branding incidents and branding fire stories for whatever interest you may find in them.

A small boy of the automobile era, knowing the co-author of this book to be an authority on brands and branding irons, rode a borrowed horse into John Hale's yard one day, pointed to the animal's brand, and said, "Mr. Hale, will you read the license number on this horse for me?"

Perhaps the most interesting ranch family you could meet nowadays would be that of George Cline, cattle king of the Tonto Basin. It is told that Mr. Cline's dad got stirred up a little when he was eighty-five years old and beat the devil out of a man half his age. George himself, a man of excellent stature, was world champion calf tier in the early 1920's. He had been very busy one week burning his Cross Seven

$$+7$$

on several hundred cows, when he had a flareup of his old trouble, tonsillitis. As soon as he could he went in to town to have the tonsils taken out.

The doctor stretched George in his big patient's chair, and reached for one of those peculiar gadgets holding a silver wire loop with which the tonsil is caught and squeezed off. George saw the loop and, his mind on branding work, lay back and mumbled through the tool in his throat, "Do you think you can catch 'em the first throw, doc?"

Ross Santee, the well known cowboy artist-author, tells that Art Sanders had a little trouble up at Globe, Arizona, one day. Art was a brand inspector when Ross was branding cows for the Cross S outfit. In the rear of one of the saloons at Globe was a toilet door carved with dozens of brands. Seemingly every cowhand for twenty years had come in there, had seen all the different brands and forthwith had been inspired to carve on his own if not already present. It was a matter of intense pride.

"We sent Art Sanders, the brand inspector, in to 'inspect' those brands," Santee says, "and when he sat down, his old hog-leg pistol, which he always wore, accidentally went off and branded Art himself! It shot just as he caught sight of the door. The bullet went through the fleshy part of his leg, doing no permanent harm but starting a legend that will last a long time."

Bill Barkley of the Quarter Circle U told this story at a branding fire powwow one night, and swore it was true.

As every rancher knows, rawhide stretches when wet and shrinks radically as it dries. One day Bill and his dad had a team of horses hitched to a light wagon with rawhide harness. Six miles from home a rain fell on them in midafternoon.

Realizing it was safest to get out of the washes, which fill quickly, and not wanting to retard the horses, Bill and his dad quickly unhooked the harness tugs, jumped on the animals and hastened the six miles to their barn. There, Bill noticed that he had failed to unhook one tug from the wagon. He hung up the harness on a peg and went into the house.

Next morning the sun came up bright, and about noon the wagon came in.

An old-time Texas cow man recently made the remark that he had voted for only one Republican in all his life. Asked why he broke over that time, he replied, "I was on a jury and voted to hang the defendant."

The menu provided by the cook at one big roundup and branding spree several years ago grew so monotonous that the foreman threatened to kill the cook unless he made a change. The cook left his chuck wagon that night after supper, rode a long way in to town, got a grocer out of bed and made a purchase, and rode back in time to prepare breakfast for the boys. As a breakfast dessert he served a new-fangled concoction called Jello. The boys all ate it, wearing various expressions of curiosity and contempt. When the meal was over, the cook spoke to the foreman.

"Well, how'd you like that there Jello, hah?"

"Jello be damned!" barked the foreman. "I'd just as soon put a funnel in my mouth and run against the wind!"

The following remark, showing what is always uppermost in a cattleman's mind, was made by a ranch father to his boy who had just reached maturity:

"Son, you can take your money and buy a car, but in the spring that car won't have a calf."

They called the mustang Blue until he threw Curly so high. After that they named him Blue Heaven.

A rancher in New Mexico, says Jack Speiden, applied for a federal loan, and listed among his assets seven cattle guards. The federal loan agency wrote back: "Inasmuch as you seek a readjustment of finances you must cut down your pay-roll first. Discharge five of those guards, as two should be ample to care for the number of cattle you have."

(A cattle guard, of course, is a contrivance of wood and steel, to keep cows from passing through a fence along a highway or railroad.)

One entirely sensible opinion in the matter of range cruelty is that of the Oregon youth who on his first ranch job was ordered to brand a yearling bull. At the first scorch of hair the bull hauled off (the boy's own phrase) and kicked out four of the brander's front teeth (which were still in Oregon when the story was told years later in New Mexico). The bull knocked him over, kicked to its feet and dragged him with the rope through the branding fire and onto several red-hot irons, ran bellowing away leaving the boy with several large burns, a per-

manent flaw in his pronunciation and a permanent aversion to
the cruelties of branding!

T. J. "Buck" Arnold, now an attorney at Houston, Texas,
recalls a similar incident, the telling of which is likely to be his
contribution whenever Houston lawyers get together for cow
talk. "Papa and I," says Buck, "were branding some calves with
the old A iron, which was the letter A on the end of a wagon
rod used as a handle. The A broke off and was flipped with the
hot handle near a tree, for future repairs.

"At this moment Jim Connell, a negro who had been sick,
limped out of the house and sat down lazily to lean against that
same tree and watch the work. Nigger Jim chanced to use the
hot A for a cushion.

" 'WHOOP!' he yelled, and had leaped to his feet and was
running before Papa or I could blink.

"Jim had been virtually an invalid, but after that show of
energy Papa promptly put him back to work. The iron doubtless would have left a permanent A on a white man's rump, but
it only scorched black Jim a little."

"Rec'lect th' time when I had a foreman named T. C. Wattrous, and he got hisself in some serious predicament with a
steer and a hot iron," says Bob Ostrander of El Paso, telling his
favorite true story.

"This Wattrous was a good man. He could do more work
than any two hands I had. But he was proud some, and bragged
a right smart.

"One day the boys was all busy, making steers of bulls and
givin' blackleg shots and branding and such, when we heard
Watt let out a yell.

"He shouted to high heaven. We thought he was kilt. He was in a bad way, as a matter of fact. He had been brandin' a right good-sized critter without tying his legs together. He could do that sometimes. Jest get the critter down while yore horse holds the lasso right, and hold his legs crossed and tight with one hand whilst you slap on the iron with the other hand.

"Wattrous, he had been doing it right along, but this critter bellered and snatched hard when the iron burnt him. He got loose from Watt, scrambled up, then tripped and fell.

"When he come down this time, Watt hisself was on the bottom, and the hot iron was right under Watt's rump!

"The pony had drawed back to keep the rope tight, like he is trained, and there Watt was with a young steer on top of him and the iron on the bottom! I cain't blame him for howling, but you cain't blame us for laughing, neither. It took Watt a month to git over that burn. He's the only man I ever see branded by a steer."

Tip Arnold of Henderson, Texas (brother of Buck, quoted above, and of the co-author here), branded cows for years around San Angelo, Texas, and has today one of the richest stores of funny cowboy stories any man could possibly have. It is worth ten dollars and a year-old filly just to sit on a rock with Tip and hear him talk for one hour. His speech is rich not only with fact and legend but with incomparable idiom of the range, an idiom which defies all authors who would reproduce it in print, for its charm in large measure is that of mimicry and vocal inflection.

"I wish you had been with me at the Texas Centennial Exposition in Dallas," Tip wrote the co-authors here. "They had a fine collection of branding irons, finest I ever saw. One I recognized right off was used by a crude old-timer named Winfield Scott, W. F. Scott.

"Winfield never saw a school functioning in his life, but he knew the open range from Dallas to Montana, and he amassed a great fortune. He could not sign his name, but he would scrawl out something that looked more like

W⅂Ƨ

than W. F. S., and it passed for his initials at western banks. That also was his brand, and it was famous because it was worn by so many thousands of cows. He was just a very humble, simple old fellow who would go in a pen and buy a thousand steers and scrawl his brand on a check good for fifty thousand dollars that his secretary had made out for him, then take a chew of stringy green tobacco, spit about fifteen feet, straddle old Choctaw and jog forty miles to the Pecos brakes and stop for his first breath. He became very rich and was boss of a string of banks as well as a string of ranches. He had an interest in banks all the way to Chicago, although he never had much to do with them in person. It was hard to get him out of the saddle, or to catch him off the range. One year, though, a big convention of western bankers finally got him roped and corralled, and forced him to attend his first highfalutin' banquet inside a hotel.

"It so happened that most of the bankers present were college graduates, and the slick-faced master of ceremonies himself was a college professor. This Mr. Chairman forced old Winfield Scott to make his first speech. He asked Winfield what he, a rough-and-tumble cowman, thought about college bred men. Old Scott stood up.

" 'Well sir,' he said, earnestly, 'I'm all for 'em. They make the best servants I can hire.' "

Tip Arnold also relates the strange circumstances surrounding the naming of a town in West Texas, although this story is likely to be heard anywhere out West.

The beautiful plains country holding Palo Duro Canyon was owned by some rich easterners, one of whom had a very beautiful daughter. She made frequent visits to ranch headquarters, and on one occasion she was riding with some cowboys and complained of being tired.

She put spurs to her horse and galloped back toward home about a mile. But she did not reckon with the far-seeing quality of Texan eyes, trained on the flat open prairie. In an urgent hurry, she suddenly reined to a halt, jumped off her horse.

"My God!" exclaimed one of the cowboys, staring. "If she ain't in plain view!"

Later the cowboy married her, founded a town on that spot and named it Plainview. It is a thriving town today.

S. Omar Barker of New Mexico tells about the two roaming cowboys who came to a chuck wagon while the cook was absent. Hungry, they probed among his pans and bags and made themselves a meal, then for devilment they found a pair of the cook's pants and burned this "We ate" brand in the seat of them: WE8

A while later a third hungry wanderer came in, found the cook still absent, made himself a free meal and added another brand to the pants: ME2

When the cook finally returned he saw his branded pants and exploded. Hungry men are welcome to a meal, but to have insulted the cook whose grub fed them was too much. The cook replaced his apron with a six-shooter, rounded up a hoss and disappeared. He was gone for almost a week, but he came back satisfied with his revenge. One by one he had run down the jokers, pulled his gun on them, tied them with a lasso so they would dangle feet up from a tree, and forcefully branded their own trousers without the formality of removing them. The brand which his running iron made was "Three Too Wise", like this:

3YY

Marion Peters of Midland, Texas, has a hobby of collecting accurate drawings of cattle brands. Marion wrote one day to Will Rogers, famous cowboy-actor, asking Will to send a correct copy of the J4 brand used by Will's father, Clem Rogers. Will gladly complied, adding this note to the paper:

"I never heard of a guy wanting a cow's autograph before. I'm surprised you didn't write direct to the cow."

An old whanghide from Colorado finally talked some woman into marrying him, the boys up there tell, and he felt the wedding should be done up according to range custom and law. If he acquired a cow or heifer, he would naturally brand her the first thing. So he naturally took his branding iron—a Diamond Cross—to the church with him that wedding day. The preacher, no less than the bride, was appalled.

"My son!" his reverence objected. "You cannot brand the woman you love, as you would a cow!"

"How come I cain't?" the bridegroom demanded.

"I'm how come," the lady herself explained, belligerently. "You just let me ketch you tryin' it!"

He was a he-man, right enough, but she was something of a he-woman. She'd weigh out around a hundred and eighty pounds of good firm meat.

"Well, uh—"

The groom's mouth dropped open. He was ill at ease. The delighted wedding guests were staring.

"You c'n compromise and brand my suitcase," the lady conceded then, "but that there's all."

He compromised.

When the after-wedding feast was on, a shrewd cowpuncher stood up at one end of the table to toast the happy couple. He quoted this historic rhyme:

"A wedding is the greatest place
For folks to go and learn.
He thought that she was his'n
But he found that he·was her'n."

2.

The same cowboys who have been squatting with you around the branding fire—stirred up after nightfall to keep you warm before bedtime—will switch from the ridiculous to the sublime on little or no provocation. The funniest branding story may be followed immediately by an apt quotation from Shakespeare or from the Bible itself. More often when the cowboy slips from humor into sentiment he begins to sing, and very few of his songs are of any musical or classical value. The better ones have been written and composed not by him, but for him and about him, by fellows whose range seldom extends beyond the Hudson River and whose knowledge of brands is limited to the N.B.C. or C.B.S. which they see stamped on radio microphones.

Col. Edward Wentworth, now with Armour & Company, recently sent the following Bible quotation to the monthly bulletin issued by the Arizona Cattlemen's Association. It is from the 39th chapter of Job, verses 19 to 25, and reads:

> Hast thou given the horse strength? Hast thou clothed his neck with thunder? Canst thou make him afraid as a grasshopper? The glory of his nostrils is terrible. He paweth in the valley, and rejoiceth in his strength: he goeth on to meet the armed men. He mocketh at fear, and is not affrighted; neither turneth he back from the sword. The quiver rattleth against him, the glittering spear and the shield. He swalloweth the ground with fierceness and rage: neither believeth he that it is the sound of the trumpet. He saith among the trumpets, Ha, ha; and he smelleth the battle afar off, the thunder of the captains, and the shouting.

Col. Wentworth also sent in Shakespeare's tribute to the horse, taken from "Venus and Adonis", lines 289 to 300:

> Look, when a painter would surpass the life,
> In limning out a well-proportion'd steed,
> His art with nature's workmanship at strife,
> As if the dead the living should exceed;
>   So did this horse excel a common one
>   In shape, in courage, colour, pace and bone.
>
> Round-hoof'd, short-jointed, fetlocks shag and long,
> Broad breast, full eye, small head and nostril wide,
> High crest, short ears, straight legs and passing strong,
> Thin mane, thick tail, broad buttock, tender hide:
>   Look, what a horse should have he did not lack,
>   Save a proud rider on so proud a back.

Here are two others of the serious type loved by ranch folk, sent in by Carlos Ronstadt, who did not write them and who could not give the authors' names, but which admittedly "hit the spot" with him:

ODE TO A HORSE

Oh, horse, you are a wondrous thing,
No horns to honk, no bells to ring.
No license buying every year
With plates to stick on front and rear.
No sparks to miss, no gears to strip;
You start yourself, no clutch to slip.
No gas bills mounting every day,
To steal the joy of life away.

Your inner tubes are all O.K.
And, thank the Lord, they stay that way.
Your spark-plugs never miss and fuss,
Your motor never makes one cuss.
Your frame is good for many a mile,
Your body never changes style.
Your wants are few and easily met,
You've something on the auto yet.

THE HORSE'S PRAYER

To thee, my master, I offer my prayer. Feed me, water and care for me, and when the day's work is done provide me with shelter, a clean, dry bed and stall wide enough for me to lie down in comfort. Talk to me. Your voice often means as much to me as the reins. Pet me sometimes, that I may serve you the more gladly and learn to love you. Do not jerk the reins and do not whip me when going up hill. Never strike, beat or kick me when I do not understand what you want, but give me a chance to understand you.

Watch me, and if I fail to do your bidding see if something is not wrong with my harness or my feet.

Examine my teeth when I do not eat. I may have an ulcerated tooth, and that, you know, is very painful. Do not tie my head in an unnatural position or take away my best defense against flies and mosquitoes by cutting off my tail.

And finally, oh, my master, when my useful strength is gone do not turn me out to starve or freeze or sell me to some cruel owner to be slowly tortured and starved to death; but do thou, my master, take my life in the kindest way and your God will reward you here and hereafter. You will not think me irreverent if I ask this in the name of Him who was born in a stable. Amen.

By far the majority of cowboy poems as of cowboy songs have to do with *my gal* and *my mother* and *my old hoss* and *graves on the lone prairee-e-e-e* and such topics. Of the very few branding poems we could find, the following two, used by kind permission of the authors, are representative:

THE RUNNIN' IRON

I have kept this runnin' iron that an old friend gave to me.
Many weary miles it travelled onderneath a cowboy's knee.
Through the sun and rain of summer, through the winter's rain
    and snow,
It was fastened to his saddle almost everywhere he'd go.

It has been upon a night hoss, it was flung beneath a shed.
It has laid out in the starlight on the saddle by his bed.
You can know without my sayin' it was built to run a brand,
But it broke a trail through cactus, out there on the desert sand.

It's been close behind a long ear when he made the gravel fly,
Racin' through the rocks and timber fer a space to ketch and tie.
It would knock out heavy gravel that got in a hoss's feet,
And to finish off a rattler it was mighty hard to beat.

You can see without half tryin' that this instrument would hurt.
It would help subdue a broncho if you didn't have a quirt.
I don't say he hunted trouble, but I sorter think he might,
Jest have used this runnin' iron fer to even up a fight.

It has rode upon his saddle through the cold and through the heat.
It's been held above a fire while he grilled a piece of meat;
Fer its owner was a cowboy, by which reason I suppose,
There's a heap of little secrets that the runnin' iron knows.

—By Bruce Kiskaddon.

MY MAN'S BRAND

I want my man
To have a brand
So all the world
Will know it's sand
In his git-up.

Not highfalutin'
Talk nor shootin'
Off at the mouth
Gits anywhere
In this old world.
It's his kind ways
And busy days
That makes me glad
To give my thanks
That I'm his girl.

I'm glad my man
Has such a brand
So all the world
Can know it's sand
In his git-up.

—By Mrs. Sebastian Brooks
of the Double Diamond Ranch.

Research for this volume "inspired" one of its authors, ranch-reared, to have a fling at branding poetry himself. After great labor the metre at least seemed passable. Elizabeth Quillin, daughter of ex-Governor John C. Phillips of Arizona, and a talented pianist, liked the poem's rhythm and so composed music for it. During the World's Championship Rodeo in Phoenix this year Bob Creamer loosened his new purple silk neckerchief, pushed his Stetson away back, and with his excellent baritone tied right into

THE BRANDING SONG [1]

Ho-o-o-o for the days on the range!
Rollicking days, frolicking days,
Out on the open range.
Cows on the run in the shimmering sun—
The echo of hoofs that are pounding;
Men who take parts with their joyous hearts
To wilderness music resounding.
Rollicking days, frolicking days,
Days on the western range.
Hear you the swish of the lariat's loop?
The throw! The catch! The jubilant whoop
Of the cowboy whose daring and generous sharing
Of work and of pleasure bring joy to the range—
Ho-o-o-o for the western range!

Ho-o-o-o for the days on the range!
Rollicking days, frolicking days,
Out on the open range.
All the men tanned by the sun and the sand,
Their deep voices loud in demanding
Irons from the fire—whoever can tire
Of the zest and excitement of branding?

[1] The Branding Song is copyrighted 1939 by Oren Arnold and Elizabeth Quillin, and all rights are reserved. Used here by special permission.

Rollicking days, frolicking days,
Days on the open range.
Monogram burned on the maverick's hide.
A bawl! A shout! "Get up and ride!"
Then the lasso is swinging again to the singing
Staccato of hoofs and of spurs on the range.
Ho-o-o-o for the western range!

When Bob was done, the crowd whooped and hollered so that he had to sing it for them again, and during that week a dozen requests for other performances came in. Next month some cowboys were overheard singing it around a branding fire in California, and not long after that some dude orchestra in Los Angeles was playing and singing it over the radio. The orchestra was stealing it, of course, but no matter; their use of it amounted to more applause. The relatively unimportant little piece is evidence again that the American public, as well as the cowboys themselves, enjoy anything based on the legend of brands and ranching.

CHAPTER XIV

"I REMEMBER WHEN"

A LETTER from the President of the United States doubtless would cause a flurry of excitement in any average office, school, or household, but we'll bet a bob-tailed bull it wouldn't be half as interesting—nor as hard to get—as a letter from Hades Temple or Give-a-Damn Starr. Uncle Hades can remember Robert E. Lee. Old Man Starr had gray hair in 1900. Neither of them yet shows any signs of dying, and neither bothers often to take pen and paper in hand.

A while ago, though, Uncle Hades did leave the ranch and come in to town for a legal matter, which took him up a slick-slidin' (his own phrase) elevator to the fourteenth floor of a skyscraper and right on into a big lawyer's office. Six other people were waiting to see the lawyer, and three businesslike young lady stenographers guarded the lawyer's private door. Uncle Hades played deaf; he *is* slightly deaf now, and he uses it to advantage. He pretended not to hear a damned thing the frowning stenographers said to him, he just strode right on through the reception room and opened the inner door. When he saw his lawyer friend, he whooped and shouted loudly enough to be heard half a mile away:

"Hi, George, you young stud horse! How are ye? Hanh? How's yore Pa?"

George, fortunately, was a smart lawyer. He dropped all other matters and gave his day to Uncle Hades. By mid-afternoon he had Uncle Hades primed up with town grub and sociability so that the old cuss was rememberin' and talking freely, and he had his best stenographer just outside the door taking down everything Uncle Hades said. She typed it all out like a letter—we expect she edited out most of the profanity and indelicate words—and then she and George read it to the old man. He was delighted. He felt honored that George should give him so much time and attention. He was tickled to hear his own thoughts and words and reminiscences read back to him. He felt more important than he'd felt in a long, long time. He put his scrawly signature on the bottom of three copies of the letter and, when George asked him, said George could publish it in the newspapers or anywhere he wanted to. But George didn't call the newspapers, he called the co-authors of this book. We think we have a scoop.

We have necessarily picked the high spots about brands and branding from his long, rambling discourse:

"Yes sir, now you take the X S brand, George. You know how it happened to be? Well, I'll tell you. It come from the excess cattle a rustler thought all his neighbors had. Pretty slick, hanh?

"I remember when a rustler name of Burley come into our community. He was a sanctimonious devil, went to church and prayed and all such, and put a cross on his cows. Now I believe in church and the good Lord, but I can't put up with no man what spits in His face. This Burley, he had a runnin' ir'n and he crossed up more'n two thousand head of young stock before anybody ever got on to him. He stole from four or five outfits, burned a holy cross on every unbranded critter he could drop his rope onto. We got hep to him at spring roundup. Somebody with a good eye for numbers seen that Burley had around two hundred calfing cows, but around five hundred right young branded calves. Cows don't have twins and triplets hardly any to speak of. We buried Mr. Burley under a wooden cross.

"Redskins took out after Mr. and Missus Morris when they come into the Mescalero Apache country. Them Mescaleros was unfitten to be let live any time, but Morris was a mind to leave 'em strictly alone, hoping they would do him the same honor. They saw him coming, though, and took out after him and his wife, and they all had quite a set-to there until some more whites heard the commotion and rescued Morris and his wife. When it was over, Morris found a tomahawk stuck in the side of his wagon. Some redskin had slung it at Missus Morris. Morris said it was a good omen because the redskin had missed, so he pitched in and put up him a log house right there, bought a few heifers and set in to raising cows. We admired his spunk. When he had to start branding, he drawed out himself a toma-hawk brand, like this: . The Morrises done right well, too. Some sons of him and Missus Morris is still living and still ranching.

"Yep, there was plenty of Indian brands. Broke arrows and bows and arrows and arrow p'ints and tomahawks and feathers was about the most used, I'd say. They'd go like this, George— you smooth 'em out with yore pencil, eh? . . . That's right. That'n was run by the McCreedys, and this big fat arrow point by Bettendorff brothers, until they both got drowned in a river crossing. Yep, they was with a bunch of us moving some stock up trail, and we come to a wide spot in a stream. Where it was wide it didn't look so swift and so we set in to swim the stock acrost, but the Betterdorff boys got mixed up with a bunch of wild old steers and some dead trees and down they went, one trying to save the life of the other. We sent four riders down stream and they fished out their bodies that evening and buried them and then caught up with us before breakfast and drunk two, three cups of coffee and rode right on with the herd without no rest. The Fat Arrow is used now by two, three other outfits.

"Sometimes you can see how brands sort of regulate the thinking of a whole town. There'll be the Bar A Bar grocery store, the Bar A Bar garage, and the Bar A Bar saloon. I hear tell El Paso has an S N A theatre but I don't know what outfit runs it.[1] Of course some towns themselves are named for brands. There's Two Dot, Montana, and Spur, Texas, I remember. And there's a street in Carey, Wyoming, named CY street for the brand of the big Carey Brothers ranch.

"Once at a branding I seen two ranchers take to fighting about their brands. Both of them was bosses, owned their outfits. They'd been squatting there heating their ir'ns with some others, and between calves they'd get to drinking and squabbling. According to what we could hear of their talk, one of them said his brand stood for more than the other'n's did because his was the United States flag. He made it this way, with a stamp ir'n:

It was a good enough brand, but being a flag didn't make it no better than the next fellow's. Anyway they took to fists, and then one of them grabbed up his hot ir'n right out of the fire.

---

[1] The theatre Mr. Temple had in mind doubtless was the Essanay at El Paso, a name which did originate from initials S and A, but which has no ranch connotation.

It was shining red. The other man grabbed his, and they had a genu-wine set-to. They slung at each other and jabbed around like soldiers with swords. Seems like both of them knew how hot an ir'n could be, and both was more afraid of hot ir'ns than of fists. A cowboy run up on his horse, jumped off and pitched in to help his boss out. That started a rush. All the hands dropped their work and run in to start fighting. I mean, them two ranches, the United States Flag and the other one, which was the Saddle Bags, drawed like this:

∞

There was eight Saddle Bags and eleven Flags, counting the bosses. One Saddle Bags had out a knife he'd been cutting bulls with, so he just pitched in to cut up some Flags if he could. I wasn't on either side, and there was four, five other outfits at that roundup, but before the rest of us could get together and go up there them two had done considerable damage to one another. A man, Flag he was, got his face all cut open from his mouth right around to the neck; his face sort of dropped open on that side. I remember the Flag cook sewed it up like he would a torn pair of pants before we got him in to a doctor. One other Flag was laid out cold. Two or three men had littler cuts and some had burns from the bosses' branding ir'ns. There wasn't any more branding or other work done that day. It took all the rest of us to hog-tie and hold down the two outfits that wanted to fight. Men can be damned fools about a brand or anything else, George, let me tell you!"

The Honorable O. D., alias "Give-a-Damn", Starr wrote his letter because we threatened to leave any mention of his brand out of this book unless he did write to us! He is an old and respected friend, and we knew he couldn't withstand such pres-

sure, even though writing was a task. Mr. Starr has been a
talker, not a writer. His unique nickname grew out of his frequent use of it as an expletive or an attitude; no matter what
situation came up in his long life, no matter what danger was
impending, O. D. Starr could be expected to snap, "I don't give
a damn!" It was said that he, like many another cowboy, would
charge hell with a bucket of water, although nobody ever knew
him to do a sneaking or dishonest thing.

"A branding iron, son" (we are forced here to correct some
of his spelling and grammar), "is to a rancher what a sceptre"
(he spelled it skepter) "is to a king. It don't mean nothing itself,
but it stands for a powerful lot. I don't mean no rancher ever
waves it around or wears it on his belt. He'd be a dam fool to
do that. I mean he uses it on his stock and it means what he aims
to do in life. Most of the time.

"You see a young man in town start out. Well, he may
decide to get himself rich by working up in a store and become
the owner and live in a big house and wear a coat with flaps
like a dam scissor-tail bird. Well, that's his way of getting along.
He ties to the name of his store. It makes more difference to
him when he sells his trademark on a drove of women's female
pants than it does to me when I git my old five-pointer burned
on a drove of heifers' hips. Or as much.

"I don't know what to tell you boys about brands. I could
name a thousand, I guess. From sea to mountains. Tom
Decrow's brand was a ship anchor" (he spelled it anker) "because Tom once drove a ship down on the Gulf. A lot of the
range boys didn't know what an anchor was at first. They
called it a Double Fishhook until Tom spread the word around.
You know about the old I D A Bar brand, which the boys
called IDA On a Rail because the bar was under the letters.

Jinglebob John Chisum [1] branded thousands of calves with a long straight rail running from shoulder to tail. No rustler could do much trying to burn over that, without making people suspicion him. Some fellow did change it a little, thisaway: _____⌒_____ . The boys got to calling it Bug On a Rail, or Knot On a Rail. And I know you boys have heard of the H C L. That means high cost of living in town as well as out here, I reckon. It's been used for a brand by ranchers who had to buck it. T A X is another one which means the boss had money troubles.

"I remember a story which is more truth than story. A ranch woman was learning her little boy to say his A B C's. She drawed an A and says, now sonny this is an A. She drawed a B and said, this is a B. She drawed a C and told him it was a C. She drawed a D and told him it was a D. But the boy was quick under the hat. He looked up and said, 'Maw, you can't fool me any more. That's not no D, that's Mr. Duncan's brand.' It's truth because many an old boy raised in a saddle learned all the letters he ever learned by seeing them in cattle brands."

By no means all the authorities on range lore are rough old-timers. Few of the old cowboys, in fact, realize that they have lived a significant part of America's youth; they were too close to the trees to see the forest. Best authority of all is a man or woman who has had generous first-hand association with cattle raising, and then has moved on up the broader cultural scale.

One of the latter in Wyoming has kindly granted permission to reproduce pertinent excerpts from one of his letters:

[1] Not to be confused with Jess Chisholm, another famous cattleman of the old days.

"DEAR JOHN:

"The teaching profession will be the loser for your having deserted it, but probably insurance will benefit in proportion. Will this give you more time to ride your branding hobby? I hope so. You must not discount the value of the research you are doing there. It is a work that will live after you, provided you arrange for the public to share the knowledge you attain. I heard your broadcast over the national radio chain. It was too sketchy, due of course to time limitations, but I imagine it was the first introduction millions of Americans ever had to our range heraldry.

"I sat on the rail with the cowboys at the Pendleton Roundup and garnered a few bits which might interest you, and again here at the big Cody Stampede. They use Indians more up here. Why don't the Arizona rodeos have more redskins in them? Your state has most Indians of all.

"I learned that the United States Cavalry formerly branded its horses on their front hoofs, instead of using numerals on the shoulder, as now. Did you know that?

"There was some discussion about the place of branding on cattle, too. All the older hands said that the left hip is the most used spot, and that agrees with what you once told me and what I have observed. Brands also are burned on the jaw, neck, shoulder, side, thigh, or breeching, to a lesser extent, of course. Purebred show stock sometimes is marked with small numerical brands near the base of the horns. I didn't know that until this week. I suppose it doesn't matter in the long run; a man can brand where he chooses. The mark made by the glowing pencil is written indelibly. Water, wind or weather won't erase it.

"A rancher selects his brand with more care than a mother

uses in naming her baby. Once he has it, he brands everything, including his reputation. R. T. Jones became Wagonrod Jones; W. C. Duncan became Hayhook Duncan; B. H. Campbell became Barbecue (Bar B Q) Campbell; J. C. Cook became Lazy J Cook. Every week new brands are being recorded, but the really unique and original ones belong to history, it seems to me. Many of those recorded now are duplicates of those created twenty, forty to sixty years ago. Cutest one I have seen recently (it may not be new, however) was this:

"It was correctly called the L In A House, but the cowboys promptly dubbed it Hell In A House. And here is a fancy one which the boys call the Japso brand:

"I respectfully suggest that your book explain among other things just how brands are registered. Not many people know it is almost the same as registering a car, except that a car registry need not be advertised.

"I heard the same talk of cattle thievery at Pendleton and Cody as you report from Mesa. The rubber-tired rustlers seem to be more active than the old mounted species, and there is less to be done about it. I don't think the modern rustler bothers to alter brands much because it isn't necessary. Probably he wouldn't be as deft at it as the old-timer was. I remember that Webb in 'The Great Plains' said, 'The cattle thief was skilled in forgery, using a hot iron for a pen and a live cowhide for parchment. He was not only a criminal but an artist.'

"It seems to me that the modern rustler is a more despicable character than the old one, a more sneaking, contemptible kind. The old hoss thief or cow thief had to take his chances, and would fight when pressed, riding like the wind and risking his neck at every turn. The modern sneak doesn't risk much of anything.

"Possibly my feeling in that matter is due to a love of horses. You know I'm still a horse fancier, John. The horse is not fully appreciated in this country. Bringing him here is one debt we owe the Spanish pioneers. In just a few decades the horse lifted the American Indians from a race of plodding footmen to a race of swift riders. The change was more radical than that effected on Whites when the steam engine came along.

"Any man who *rides* achieves a magnificence, a superiority to his fellow beings. You remember how no genuine cowboy would ever walk if he could possibly avoid it. You remember too that it was the ranchers who came into the Southwest on horseback and made a hospitable country out of the most inhospitable country one could imagine, defying drought, cactus thorns, reptiles, loneliness, savage Indians, isolation. Footmen couldn't have done that, nor could our modern soft-brained motorists. In those pioneer days a branding iron identified a rancher's property, and the shooting iron forced recognition of that identification.

"Under separate cover I am sending you a beaded necktie. You can wear it when you want to show off, as a dude would. It is the only necktie I ever saw covered with beads, and it was made by an Indian squaw here at the rodeo. You will see how she has beaded in about twenty cattle brands.

"Best personal regards—

LAWRENCE DALE."

Of quite different interest is this letter from a woman in Seattle, Washington:

"DEAR MR. HALE:

"I've been talking to a very interesting old buyer and line rider from Montana and South Dakota. He worked for the Shadey Cattle Company of Chicago, one of the larger buyers of the early 90's. This company's brand was the Flying U. Their concentration range was in western South Dakota in the Belle Fourche River region. They bought thousands of two-year-olds in Texas and sent them to South Dakota before finally shipping to Chicago. Their biggest buys were from the.L F D ranch just south of Dallas, Texas. The L F D people were the first Texas raisers to improve the Hereford strain by breeding for short horns. The company also bought H O, C Y, and Turkey Track brands for Chicago market. These steers would weigh about four hundred and fifty pounds when bought in Texas at three cents a pound. They would be kept in South Dakota until they weighed about eleven hundred pounds. Two dollars was added to the selling price of each animal for cow hand hire.

"Eighteen hours a day was the ranch hands' working time. On roundups ten horses were allowed per man. Saddles used were from Galloping Frazier of Pueblo, Colorado, and from Cogshell of Miles City.

"This old man was sent to Mexico to buy horses for use during the World War. Accompanied by a lieutenant and sergeant, he spent several months in Mexico. One of the most common brands used for both cattle and horses there they found to be the Terrazas brand.

"The Shadey Cattle Company did not counter-brand any of their Texas cattle, but branded on the right shoulder with their Flying U.

"I spent three years on John French's ranch just north of

Beaumont, Texas, 1904–06. There were thousands of acres of open range then. Our brand was H 5 2 Fleur-de-Lis:

H52Y

It was a very cruel brand. It always took three irons and sometimes four or more.

"All of these ranchers used the running iron, although Texas has passed a law forbidding the use of this iron. Cowboys making the fleur-de-lis would invariably run the lower part into one very broad, deep burn, and many times deep scars resulted.

"Each of Mr. French's children at birth was given a heifer— the start of a herd. Males were either sold or traded for heifers or cows by the father until each child was old enough to take care of his own herd. Mrs. French had her own herd, too. Thus John French, his wife, and each of their children owned separate brands, the wife's and children's all being built on John's original H 5 2 Fleur-de-Lis. Here is the succession, with each owner, to show how complicated this brand became:

H52Y	H 5 2 Fleur-de-Lis. John French
H52Y	H 5 2 Fleur-de-Lis Under Bar. Mrs. John French
H52Y	H 5 2 Fleur-de-Lis Double Under Bar. Nina French
H52Y	H 5 2 Fleur-de-lis Over Bar. Avey French
H52Y	H 5 2 Fleur-de-Lis Double Over Bar. Homer French
H52Y	H 5 2 Fleur-de-Lis Through Bar. Lonnie French
H52Y	H 5 2 Fleur-de-Lis Double Through Bar. Burton French

"When it was necessary to counter-brand, this brand was crossed out like this: H52Y

"It was a custom on this ranch that every one who stayed any length of time had to brand a calf. They were shown how to throw a calf and hold it. It was then up to them. Throw it, hold it, brand it! I was a wreck after my experience. The poor calf's eyes came way out, his mouth was open, the tongue was way out, and oh—the smell of hair and that terrible frying, sizzling noise of burning!

"Our Indian brands out here in Washington are nearly all geometrical figures—circles, squares, diamonds, triangles, and all kinds of combinations of these figures, such as Circle Box and Box Diamond: ◘ ◈ . Our best known sheep brand is Circle W, owned by Bartons, raisers and packers. The brand is made thus:

"The old-timer told me that he thought a great many people had the wrong idea of big ranches. The popular idea was that the hands were one grand, rollicking, roistering, cowboy singing group with no restraints. But they were not. There was no gambling nor drinking allowed on any part of the ranges or in shelters. The small towns nearby afforded an outlet for all such entertainment.

"My work now is library reading, and through this I contact the children and learn their likes. So far I have failed to find a group that is not interested in brands. Most of the material is old and, I may say, not very interestingly arranged. I tell every group about your book coming out. Anticipation is high.

"I hope these bits of disjointed information may be of some use.

"Very sincerely,

"CORA A. RIDGWAY"

Mrs. Ridgway's good letter is indeed valuable. In its reminiscences of brand and range lore it is typical of the kind of thing one dyed-in-the-wool westerner is likely to write another, even though both are not actively in the saddle any more. Ranch talk is still "shop-talk" with them, although Mrs. Ridgway is a teacher and Mr. Hale an insurance man now. Mrs. Ridgway "remembers when." Note that she refers to the brand of the ranch where she was a guest as *our* brand. After thirty-five years or so her heart still holds that characteristic personal loyalty, even though she makes tacit admission that the H 5 2 Fleur-de-Lis was not entirely perfect.

Excerpts from the following letter are quoted in other parts of this book, where they would be more apropos of the discussion immediately at hand. It is from William Tip Arnold of Henderson, Texas, brother of the co-author here and a peppery cattleman and horse man since the 1890's.

"DEAR OREN:

"As to branding irons, I remember those at Dallas at the Centennial Exposition. They had the finest collection of irons I ever saw. It seemed to me every old-time ranch in the West was represented. The folklore and legendary tales that went to make up the irons perhaps three generations ago was told to visitors as they passed along.

"Went out next morning after I wrote that and caught six catfish from the same hook from the new lake on the ranch, one right after the other. They weighed about two pounds each. All caught in day time. Gigged fifteen big frogs too. Have just finished some pasture fences. Am starting a new brand of my own. Trading activity is slow here now, so we are not making any money. Hauled out a truck load of odds and ends for the hands.

"If you could get hooked up in Dallas and Fort Worth with some old western ranch bosses, you'd get more branding legends than I can remember. Thirty-seven years ago I was with chuck-wagons from Uvalde to the Capitan Gap, out from old Santa Fe and back to Concho headwaters, when cows had long horns. Cows, cows, cows, only cows and sheep were in evidence.

"I saw Mexicans who made it their business, and they had no other business, move in to ranch headquarters to run the branding iron ditch. I mean by this, that a ditch is dug a hundred feet long, one or two feet deep, filled with fire to make red-hot coals. Mexican experts like this tag from ranch to ranch from year to year and do little else but run a string of irons. One hundred, maybe two hundred, irons would be kept there hot and ready for call as fifty or a hundred calves would be run through the chutes in just a minute, not branded one at a time but a hundred at a time by experts, everything moving fast. It looked like confusion to an outsider, but it made sense there. I was with the Seven K and then the Bar X, which looked like this: 7K   —X . In fact brands were as common as plow points in a farm county. I was on, in, under and part of one big roundup, and have a broken nose to this day as a result, where at least a dozen brands were used on more than ten thousand head of cattle. The roundup covered a third of a million acres or better. Fifty-odd cow hands were working all the time, one bunch at night holding the herd together, another bunch by day working them.

"I have seen fifty thousand head of cattle at one time milling around the pens at San Angelo waiting their turn for a train to Chicago, Saint Jo, Saint Louis, Kansas City or Fort Worth. I was in one western midnight rainstorm where the lightning flashed along the horns of thousands of steers, and for the moment Coney Island was no brighter, and the next moment hell no darker. You can imagine what happened.

"I made lots of long drawn out trips to points mentioned, but speaking of coincidences, we were taking sixteen hundred cows to the Osage range in Indian Territory, got to Brownwood and a switch engine plowed through us from one side, killed a few cattle and caused a week's delay. This gave me time to look over Brownwood, where I saw Howard Payne College and later came back and attended for nearly two years. Funny what will send a man to hell or to college.

"At one time I saw a row over a very fierce old sagetail horse which was alleged to have been stolen. The thief was in court about it. The horse had been traded or stolen many times, and a new brand had hit him at every turn, so that his hide looked like the map of Mexico. I saw him shot by the hide inspector, and skinned so as to see whose brand hit him last. The red flesh scar is the best evidence.

"Thirty-seven years ago there existed in San Angelo a horse and mule firm named March and Thornton. Dr. John Abe March, then a power in the West, was from Mt. Enterprise, Texas, and was a close friend of our grandfather Tom Arnold. It's a shame you didn't get to know him. Dr. John Abe was my friend. I rode with him in a buggy hundreds of miles. You get to know a man in a buggy better than in a confounded automobile, although a car, I reckon, has its place. A car, a truck I mean, is better to haul stuff to the ranch than a wagon is. But a buggy is better for talking politics and for courting a girl.

When I got married I offered my girl the choice of a diamond ring or a rubber-tired buggy with a high-stepping stallion. You saw how we sashayed around in that buggy for years after our honeymoon. Do you remember that horse? Old Ernest? A big fine bay, with not a mark on him except a small brand, until that time the train scared him up at Mr. Cannon's and he plunged into the bob wire.

"I will close. Pass this letter on to Virginia.

"Yours truly,

"Tip"

It is a pleasure here to "pass the letter on to Virginia"—and to all other relatives, friends and strangers who may be interested in these reminiscences with their genuine flavor of the range.

Now, the authors have a great many other letters from ranch folk which just couldn't be included. A book has to stop somewhere, and here the back cover is already blocking us, like a box canyon wall. Inevitably some of you friends and kindly strangers are going to feel hurt because your letter is omitted or your beloved brand isn't even mentioned. Forgive us that, please.

To those disappointed ones, and to the many other ranchers and ex-ranchers who will now feel inspired to write in, please know that your information *is* important and is appreciated. Moreover, it will certainly be made available to other research workers and writers who may want to proclaim some of the good things about our land and its people.

That westerners do trouble to write about their brands and their brand stories is in itself significant. An outdoorsman ordinarily isn't much of a writer; he has to feel a strong heart urge. The willing and voluntary cooperation of so many men and women—and this applies to town and city dwellers who can also "remember when"—materially strengthens our case for the heraldry of the range.

To one and all of you—good grazing and, "So long."

THE END

NAMES OF BRANDS

1. T Over A.
2. Bar Oh, or Bar Nothing.
3. Diamond And A Half.
4. Whip.
5. Slashed Lazy S.
6. R Down R Up Connected, or Double R.
7. Lazy Y 4.
8. Spectacles.
9. Walking H.
10. Lazy Ladder.
11. Swinging V.
12. Christmas.
13. Toppling or Tilting R.
14. Five Diamonds.
15. Running M.
16. Angle A.
17. Chamber 2 Corn Cobs.
18. Drunken T.
19. Lazy J D Connected.
20. Wind Vane.
21. Buzzard On A Rail.
22. Rafter A.
23. W Diamond.
24. T Anchor.
25. Barrel.
26. Box C, or Block C.
27. Lamp Chimney.
28. 3 Lazy S.
29. Drag 9.
30. Rocking K.
31. K K K Konnected.
32. Corkscrew.
33. Barnett.
34. M Over W.
35. Seventy-Six.
36. Scissors.
37. H On T.
38. Plow.
39. Diamond E Connected.
40. Keyhole.
41. Sunrise.
42. Z Slash Z.
43. Pothooks T.
44. L G.
45. Cross Triangle.
46. Window Sash.
47. Frying Pan, or Wagon Rod.
48. Snake S.
49. Cloudy Moon.
50. Quarter-Circle V Bar.